THE
CLIFFE HILL
MINERAL RAILWAY

THE
CLIFFE HILL
MINERAL
RAILWAY

PETER outside the tarmac plant at Beveridge Lane.

Collection: *Jim Peden.*

M. H. Billington
Revised by David H. Smith

PLATEWAY PRESS

THE
CLIFFE HILL
MINERAL RAILWAY

First edition published 1974 by Turntable Enterprises, Leeds.
Second (revised) edition published 1997.

ISBN 1 871980 23 2

Printed by
Postprint, Taverner House, Harling Road,
East Harling, Norwich, NR16 2QR

Cover artwork and book design by
Roy C. Link

PLATEWAY PRESS
Taverner House, Harling Road, East Harling, Norwich, NR16 2QR

FOREWORD
by Allan C. Baker

An interest of mine in the locomotive builder and railway engineer, W. G. Bagnall Ltd., of Stafford, goes back to school boy days. In my father's collection was a copy of the firm's last and magnificent catalogue, and a series of postcards illustrating their locomotives with dimensional detail on the rear, and issued between the wars. These had come my father's way via a former employee of the Company and a fellow member of the local model engineering society.

Later, father helped the widow of the well known Stafford model engineer, John W. Bagnall, no relation to W. G., catalogue and dispose of his collection. Among John's possessions was a partly built $2^{1}/_{2}$in gauge Bagnall narrow gauge locomotive, the prototype being one of the company's famous circular firboxed patent valve gear saddle tanks, the actual prototype was an 0–4–2 on 2ft 6in gauge. This, together with a large collection of literature on the company had come into John's ownership pre-war, from Horace Lorton, one of Bagnall's Cost Office staff at the time.

Thereafter, my interest in the Company and its products has known no bounds. Father and I found Horace still living in retirement at nearby Brocton, and to our delight, only part of his collection had passed to John Bagnall, so much more came our way.

It was about this time that the Company was taken over by English Electric, and one of their first actions was to rid themselves of ISABEL. This was the Cliffe Hill locomotive the Company had bought back in 1953, to be restored and displayed at the works as a celebration of the men and locomotives the firm had built since its inception in 1875. This locomotive, so typical of the company's products had been acquired at the instigation of the then Managing Director, W. A. Smyth, a railway man for much of his life, and something of an enthusiast. Restoration, largely by the apprentices of the day was overseen by the General Manager, Harry Davies, himself Kerr Stuart trained, but a long time Bagnall employee. As related here by David, ISABEL later found her way into local authority ownership and is now on the Amerton Railway.

Cliffe Hill were loyal and early customers of Bagnall, indeed all their early locomotives came from the Castle Engine Works stable and much of their other railway equipment too. Bagnall supplied the original track work, including points, wagons, and much else and continued to do so, along with other manufacturers, over the years. Vic Betterley, Production Manager latterly at Stafford and Bagnall trained, recalls that there was rarely a time when an order of one sort or another, however small, was not going through the shops for Cliffe Hill. Of course, on occasions the little locomotives, or large parts of them, came back to the works for attention.

W. S. Edwards, Managing Director in the 1930's and 40's, and a Bagnall man from 1901 until his death in 1946, was Chief Draughtsman when the locomotive MARY and the second JACK were designed and built. He always reckoned that this type of 0-4-2 side tank was ideal for quarry work, but then I suppose he would, leading the design team at the time! However, by this time the First World War and all that meant in its aftermath, effectively put a rapid end to the continued development of narrow gauge steam railways for use in quarries and the like.

One of the very first fellow narrow gauge railway enthusiasts I corresponded with, principally on my interest in W. G. Bagnall Ltd., but also on narrow gauge railways generally, was Maurice Billington. I came across his name in some files of correspondence the Company had had with enthusiasts, and loaned to me by Bill Brooks, the last Chief Draughtsman. He had rescued them from the proverbial bonfire. A steady correspondence started, which albeit less steadily, continues today, and it was good to be able to help Maurice with the First Edition of this book. It has been a pleasure too, to assist again, not only expanding on the information for a bigger, more lavish production, but also because continuing research into the Company and its surviving records, has bought more information to light. As always, Plateway Press have done their subject justice, and it is a pleasure for me to pen these few words. The locomotives and equipment Cliffe Hill used were so typical of Bagnall, and the Preston's were "friends" of the Company for many years, as Gordon Bagnall liked to call his customers. The firm made great play of their ability to completely equip light railways and they had much success in such ventures, both in this country and world wide. Cliffe Hill too, is not a little typical of the narrow gauge railways so familiar in quarrying and allied industries in the years before the First World War.

Here then, we have the bringing together of a typical quarry narrow gauge railway and the products of one of this country's most prolific exponents of this form of transport, and one whose little locomotives find a warm place in the heart of many a narrow gauge railway enthusiast. I commend Maurice's and David's story, it is a good read and another bit of our country's industrial history so well told.

ALLAN C. BAKER

High Halden, Kent
January 1997

INTRODUCTION
To the First Edition

I first learned of the Cliffe Hill Quarry and its railway via that invaluable little guide book "Industrial Locomotives of the East Midlands" published by the Birmingham Locomotive Club in 1947.

Unfortunately at the time I was sojourned in hospital and was unable to pay a visit until 1950 when I discovered the locomotives cold and forlorn at their resting place on the spoil bank, and then, after a walk along the tramway to the sidings in the blazing sun, decided to write a brief article on the line.

Correspondence with my good friend Eric Tonks of the B.L.C.,* and later the mass of documents shown to me by Mr Peter Preston and Mr Derek Perry of the Quarry Co., convinced me that an article could not possibly do the line justice and so I embarked on writing my first book.

I admit it has taken me an inordinately long time to complete it, as each time I visited the quarry, or chatted with former employees, more details came to light and it was my intention to make the book as comprehensive as possible. Although there have been many delays and difficulties it has nonetheless given me a great deal of pleasure, particularly the conversations with the old drivers, fitters, etc. and through my visits I have come to know and love the area around Cliffe Hill and many of the people who have worked on the railway.

It is my earnest hope that those who read this account will enjoy it.

M. H. BILLINGTON

Nuneaton, Warwickshire
1973

* *Now the Industrial Railway Society.*

INTRODUCTION
To the Second Edition

My involvement with the Cliffe Hill Granite Co came about by being actively engaged in the preservation of equipment from the quarry. As a Trustee of the Brockham Museum I set about finding information on all the exhibits; PETER from Cliffe Hill was one of these. Later, when the Brockham collection was transferred to Amberley, there was a larger number of exhibits to research, but the opportunity came to complete the restoration of PETER at last, carried out by Doug Bentley and his team, after so many years. A change of lifestyle coupled with a house move several hundred miles away, means that I am no longer involved, but not before I had helped to acquire and move some former Cliffe Hill track, so that for a part of its short passenger run at the Museum, PETER can now feel very much at home! I am now on the Committee of the Narrow Gauge Railway Society which owns the locomotive.

I was very pleased to be asked by Plateway Press to revise and update Maurice Billington's history. Much of the text has been left largely as written by Maurice, but in the meantime much more has been learned about the locomotive history, and of course, the two surviving locomotives have both been moved since the first edition, and restored to working order, which called for additional chapters in the book. Modern production methods and the Plateway Press reputation for high quality mean that a bigger and better selection of photographs can be included.

I look forward to seeing ISABEL and PETER reunited at Amerton to celebrate the former's Centenary.

DAVID H. SMITH
Hebden Bridge, Yorkshire
1997

ACKNOWLEDGEMENTS

A book of this nature could not have been written without the help and advice so freely given by many people and to these we offer our sincere and grateful thanks.

The following individuals and organisations contributed to the First Edition:-

Peter McHowell Preston, Derek Perry, Fred Boulds, Fred Goodman, Bill Read, Syd Dilk, Fred Cooke, William Anderson, Alf Hayes, Joe Reynolds, Bob Woods, Mr Kibble, Doug Spence, Bill Cave, Mr Ward; all of whom were present or past employees of the Company. All those people who lived near the line and who have told me of happenings in years gone by, but whose names unfortunately I did not record.

Fellow enthusiasts, Eric S. Tonks, Ken Hartley, Mike Swift, Ron Redman, Roger West, Ted Wade, Allan Baker (W. G. Bagnall details), Rodney Weaver (E. E. Baguley details), Eric Hannen, Ray King and his late father, both of whom lived near the line and knew it well, Roy Etherington, Geoffrey Taylor, "Rich" Morris, John Townsend, Eric Cope, and Bill Woolhouse of the Lincs. Coast Light Railway.

Other useful sources of information were The English Electric Co. Ltd. (successors to W. G. Bagnall Ltd.); George Cohen, Sons & Co. Ltd.; White's Directory for 1863, 1877 & 1900; Kelly's

Directory for 1900 & 1916; Victoria County History of Leicestershire Vol. 3 pp 43 & 47; Ordnance Survey 6in Maps 1st Edition 1884/5; 2nd Edition 1903/4, and for 1929.

Thanks are also due most heartily to the staff of the County Records Office in Leicester for their patience and consideration shown to me and for enabling me to study the above directories and maps in warmth and comfort.

This revised Edition was produced with with assistance from the following:-

This revised Edition of the book has been prepared by David H. Smith, who has brought the story up to date and added the Chapters describing the rescue and preservation of both PETER and ISABEL.

Most of the revised information on locomotive history has been provided by Allan C. Baker, whose knowledge of Bagnall equipment has willingly been placed at our disposal. Allan also agreed to write the Foreword. Considerable assistance with the two "Preservation" chapters has been provided by Doug Bentley of Amberley Museum (PETER) and John Strike of the Amerton Railway (ISABEL).

Other people who have helped with information for this Edition include, Geoff Horsman, John Kimber, Andrew Neale, Jim Peden, and Mike Swift. Much of the preliminary work was done by Keith Taylorson.

The drawing of THE ROCKET were prepared for this Edition, whilst that of MARY was prepared for the first Edition and thanks are due to Ted Wade for permission to re-use it. The drawing of PETER was prepared by the late Bill Strickland and is reproduced by courtesy of the Merioneth Railway Society; and the drawing of the tipping wagon was prepared by Alan Kidner from the Howard original.

The following secondary sources were consulted in compiling this Revised Edition:-

Bagnall Locomotives – A Pictorial Album of Bagnall Narrow Gauge Locomotives		
Allan Baker & Allen Civil	Trent Valley Publications	1990
Baguley Locomotives, Rodney Weaver	Industrial Railway Society	1974
Dam Builders' Railways From Durham's Dales to the Border		
Harold D. Bowtell	Plateway Press	1994
Industrial Locomotives of Dyfed & Powys	Industrial Railway Society	1994
Industrial Locomotives of Northumberland	Industrial Railway Society	1983
Industrial Railway Record No. 54	(Magazine) Industrial Railway Society	1974
Industrial Railway Record No. 62	(Magazine) Industrial Railway Society	1975
Industrial Railway Record No.125	(Magazine) Industrial Railway Society	1991
Industrial Railway Record No.126	(Magazine) Industrial Railway Society	1991
Industrial Railway Record No.138	(Magazine) Industrial Railway Society	1994
Narrow Gauge & Industrial Railway		
Modelling Review No. 25	(Magazine) RAM Productions Ltd	1996
The Kerry Tramway, David Cox & Chris. Krupa	Plateway Press	1992
The Narrow Gauge No. 128	(Magazine) Narrow Gauge Railway Society	1990

CONTENTS

Dedicated to the late
Mr Peter McHowell Preston,
whose hospitality and enthusiasm
inspired Maurice to write this history.

CHAPTER ONE
IN THE BEGINNING

MARKFIELD IN LEICESTERSHIRE is a village which can only be glimpsed by travellers speeding north on that most picturesque section of the M1 Motorway as it climbs up from Leicester Forest East, then skirts Charnwood Forest, past Shepshed and on to Kegworth and Nottinghamshire. The fine old Church in Markfield with its lofty spire may just be seen half a mile away on the right, but they will almost certainly see on their left a large derrick crane, buildings and mounds of granite waste belonging to a large quarry and it is this which forms the subject of this book. In the 1890's it was much different, the village, it is true, has not altered a great deal except in size, but the roads, even including the main Ashby-Coalville-Leicester road (now the A50), which runs at the top of the village, were only narrow, rutted lanes used by farmer's carts and the occasional carrier; when the villagers wished to travel to Leicester or Coalville the usual method was to walk the four miles to Bardon Hill station on the Midland Railway's Burton-Leicester branch (originally the Leicester & Swannington Railway) and perforce do the same upon their return, and this pattern of travel was to suffice except for a few passengers who travelled by carrier's cart until after the Great War when Motor Buses appeared on the main road.

The area around Markfield is pleasant, rolling countryside at an elevation of approximately 600 feet and is inclined to be rather windswept. Farming is carried on and there is a small steel Container Factory in the village, but undoubtedly the main industry in the area is the quarrying of granite. The particular form of granite, found only in this small area of Leicestershire (and known appropriately as "Markfieldite"), was formed some five hundred million years ago by underground eruptions and is a very hard stone. The Romans are reputed to have used it for building their roads, and during the succeeding centuries small quarries had been opened, but it was not until the 1860's that the stone was worked on a commercial scale. The first known quarry was just behind the village, and owned by Mr Everard who later opened a much larger quarry at Bardon Hill, and in partnership with Mr John Ellis of Leicester founded the large firm which, bearing these two names of Ellis & Everard, existed for many years (the quarry still exists trading under the name Bardon Hill). The old Everard's quarry lasted some forty years but filled with water and was abandoned. However a mile to the west on the high

'Office and Staff in 1893' – from a Cliffe Hill Granite brochure published in the early 1960's The chalked lettering above the doorway reads: 'Ye Office & Staff of Ye Cliffe Hill Granite Company'. To one side is chalked: Staff – J. R. Fitzmaurice P. Preston F. Gibson.

ground of Cliffe Hill, two Birmingham businessmen had formed a partnership in the late 1870's under their names of Jones and Fitzmaurice to work the stone which was eminently suitable for making street setts and kerb stones, but this quarry, too, closed after a very few years and remained so for a decade. This quarry was acquired by Mr J. Rupert Fitzmaurice from his father on 9 May 1891, and as he needed a manager for the quarry he wrote to Mr Peter Preston who was at that time working at a quarry at Enderby (presumably for Mr Everard) offering him the position. It is recorded that the interview was held, with both parties sitting on a pile of stones and Mr Preston duly accepting the managership at the salary of £3 per week. He commenced his duties on 25 May of that year, and his initial task was to arrange for a crusher.

Mr Preston brought a millwright and a blacksmith with him from Enderby and, with the addition of some of the employees from the old quarry, set about cutting grass and digging off the topsoil to bare the rock which they started to quarry on 12 June (for some reason they must have decided against extending the original hole). A rock drill was first used on 17 June, and by 2 July a jaw crusher was installed and ready to work, powered by a steam engine built by Marshalls of Gainsborough, coupled to a Thompson boiler.

A second crusher was soon added, a licence to store and use explosives was obtained on 15 July and from then on the little quarry made good progress. The first load of stone was sold to a local farmer at 2/6d per ton, more sett makers and kerb dressers were engaged and these products were sold to the former owners of the quarry who were in the contracting business.

Rock drilling was by means of steam driven drills, the secondary drilling being done by hand. This was a tricky operation with a man and a boy working together, the boy held a short drill with both hands and the quarryman's job was to strike the drill with a sledge hammer, the boy turning the drill slightly after each blow. When a hole of sufficient depth had been drilled, the stone was split by means of plugs. Two feathers (flat pieces of steel) were placed in the hole and the steel plug, which was wedge shaped, was placed between the feathers and driven in by hammer blows until the stone split. The stone would then be broken by hand to a size of approximately 10in-12in and loaded into quarry tubs. A tally or metal label bearing the man's number was attached and these were collected when the stone was tipped into the mill and taken to the quarry foreman. A daily record of work done was prepared and sent to the office at the close of the working day. Every possible job was put on a piecework basis, and from the number of tallies received in the office and the quality of the stone loaded (stone with a brown skin was rejected and the workman who had loaded the wagon fined) the man's pay was calculated.

As mentioned earlier the stone was highly suitable for making setts and kerbs and the quarryman would sort out the stones most suitable for this purpose. The large blocks (approximately $2^1/_2$ to 3 feet long) were sent to the kerb sheds, and the smaller, squarer stones to the settmakers' sheds. The Company paid the quarryman for his stone, the kerb dresser and settmaker bought the stone from the company, worked it and then sold it back to the company again, together with the waste chippings. The reason for this rather roundabout procedure is not known, but was not uncommon in the quarrying industry, particularly in the slate quarries of North Wales where it was a common practice until recent times. Not all the jobs could be done on a piecework basis however, and the day rates varied between 4d per hour for labourers, to 5d per hour for skilled men, being graduated in d. The working day was 10 hours, and on Saturdays 5 hours were worked; in those days the lot of a quarryman was very hard indeed.

The output of stone for the first twelve months was 10,200 tons of broken stone and 630 tons of dressed stone. Delivery was effected by horse and cart, with most of the stone going to

J. R. Fitzmaurice   *Peter Preston*   *Peter L. Preston*   *Peter McH. Preston*

Directors and Chairmen of the Cliffe Hill Granite Company Limited 1891-1960. Taken from the same brochure as the photo on page one. The first two gentlemen are those shown standing in front of the office in the 1893 scene.
J. R. Fitzmaurice was the first Chairman of Directors and Peter Preston the first Manager & Secretary. He later became a Director and his son, Peter Lionel Preston took over his former posts. He in turn became both a Director and Chairman. When he died in 1954 his son, Peter McH. Preston had been joint Managing Director for two years.

Bagworth Station for transit by rail. The first really large contract was secured as early as 1892 for $^1/_4$in. clean chippings for the Patent Victoria Stone Co. Output continued to grow as further crushers were installed and to facilitate transport to the Station a traction engine was ordered in 1892 and was received in November of that year and named SANS PAREIL. It was a very strong engine capable of hauling five trailers loaded to 10 tons and cost the Company £469 from the makers, McLaren & Co. of Leeds. So successful was this engine that a second was bought in the following year.

On the 3 January 1894 the company received its first railway contract for 5,000 tons and on the 1 November in that same year, the Cliffe Hill Granite Co. Ltd. was formed. The founder of the firm (Mr Fitzmaurice) lived in Leicester and often walked to Bagworth Station to catch his train home. It is recorded that in the event of his having to wait for a train on the platform, the time would be profitably filled noting the Midland Railway's rates to different places in a special notebook.

The demand for the company's products continued to increase. After only a few years the steam traction engines were found to be inadequate and the decision was made by the board to lay a light railway of two feet gauge from the quarry to the Midland Railway's line; this to be worked by steam locomotives. It was at first considered that a line in the Bagworth direction would serve the purpose best and a firm of Coalville surveyors were engaged. The route to Bagworth would have been fairly direct though heavily graded, but Mr Breedon Everard owned much of the land over which it would have run. He did not take kindly to the idea of allowing his principal competitors to build a line and thus compete even more favourably with his own quarries, so he refused to sell or lease the land, and the Cliffe Hill Company had to settle for a route to the sidings at Beveridge Lane, nearer to Bardon Hill station. While being no longer than the Bagworth route would have been, it was much less direct, with severe gradients, and abounding in sharp curves. Negotiations with the Midland Railway were opened for the layout and construction of sidings and when these were completed, tenders were sent out to the leading builders of locomotives and equipment.

CHAPTER TWO

"ENTER THE IRON HORSE"

ONLY THREE FIRMS are known to have quoted for the supply of locomotives but they were all firms of high repute which specialised in the building of locomotives for industrial use, and between them they supplied a large proportion of those to Britain's industrial concerns. The first quote to arrive was from Manning, Wardle & Co. of the Boyne Engine Works, Leeds, on 5 June 1896 and was for an 0-4-0ST with 8in x 12in outside cylinders, copper firebox, complete with "A neat canopy of sheet iron, supported on wrought iron pillars to be fixed over the driver's footplate," the wheels would have been of 2ft 0in diameter on a wheelbase of 4ft 3in. Water capacity was to be 200 gallons and the weight in working order 11 tons – unfortunately the photograph which must have been sent with the specification has not survived.

The quarry company must have requested that a locomotive having a circular firebox be quoted for, but just why they should have asked for one of this type is not known. It was in common use then for traction engines, it was much favoured by W. G. Bagnall and of course at this time Sir Arthur Heywood was building his locomotives at Duffield Bank with this type of firebox. It was also considerably cheaper to build, but Manning, Wardle in a letter of 8 June stated that they were not quoting for that style of box, which was in their view "out of date, and not nearly so serviceable or economic … (as the standard type)". The price quoted on 5 June had been £660, but a subsequent letter of 8 September stated that "resulting from an increase in the workmen's wages, the price would have to be increased to £685, cash on delivery."

On the same date as Manning, Wardle first quoted, so did the Hunslet Engine Co., also of Leeds, and their specification described a locomotive also of the 0-4-0ST variety but with 8in x 10in cylinders. Wheels were 1ft 9in diameter on a wheelbase of 4ft, and the weight in working order was eight tons. The price for this engine "complete with lamps, tools and screw jack" was £575 delivered. A larger locomotive with $8^{1}/_{2}$in x 14in cylinders, weighing eleven tons was also suggested, but Hunslet's considered that this might prove to be a little heavy. However, James Campbell who had dictated the letter said that he would be pleased to visit the quarry "to inspect your roads and works and give you the benefit of our experience of upwards of 30 years". He also stated that "We have within the last fortnight completed a repeat order for a 2ft 0in gauge loco, rather smaller than this for your neighbours, The Groby Granite Co. Ltd." This would have been SEXTUS, Works No. 652 of 1896, which later became LADY MADCAP of the Dinorwic Slate Quarry at Llanberis in North Wales.

Mr Campbell's visit took place on 11 June and a subsequent letter and specification was sent on the following day, describing a locomotive of the makers' well known "Lilla" class (as supplied to Cilgwyn Slate Quarries, Nantlle) with 9in x 14in cylinders and 2ft 2in wheels. He (Mr Campbell) considered that this would be more suitable in view of the "1 in 20 gradient on the line, which would however require the locomotive to be worked in full gear to take a twenty ton train". The locomotive would cost £725 in complete working order and could be delivered in two months from the date of the order. The cab of the loco would have had back and side plates

Di and Saul Books

6 Bleasdale Road

Knott End-on-Sea

Poulton-le-Fylde

Lancashire

FY6 0DQ

Tel: 01253 424427

Email: sales@diandsaulbooks.co.uk

We hope you're happy with your purchase, but in the unlikely event there is a problem please don't hesitate to contact us and we promise to sort it out straight away!

CLIFFE in the shed at the quarry. Collection: Frank Jones.

removable in summer time and would have weighed 10 tons. Unfortunately, in a letter to Mr Preston dated 8 November 1897, Mr Campbell stated that "owing to a strike which caused work to be practically at a standstill for seventeen weeks, they were in such arrears that delivery could not be promised for five months after the strike was settled", but he reiterated that the small locomotive quoted on 5 June 1896 would be "of ample power to deal with a gross load of 30 tons on your worst gradient, which is stated as 1 in 49 - we note that when we last quoted, 1 in 20 was mentioned as the steepest gradient, that appears however to be eliminated now"; the price for this small engine was £590.

For some reason both Manning, Wardle and The Hunslet Engine Co. in letters, mentioned the reduction in height of the locomotive which would result if the cab was dispensed with. There was no overbridge on the line, so the reason for this is not apparent, unless of course it was intended that the locomotive would have to be capable of working under a low screen at the quarry.

It is interesting to speculate on the attractive Manning, Wardle, or Hunslet engines which might have worked at the quarry, but on 15 September 1896 a letter written personally by Mr W. G. Bagnall of the Castle Engine Works, Stafford, was sent to confirm a verbal offer by Mr E. E. Baguley, the Company's Chief Draughtsman, made the previous day. In this he offered locomotives, rails and turntables on very favourable terms thus: "Engines and Turntables £300 cash paid through Messrs Jones & Fitzmaurice, the remainder to be paid over a period of three years." From this it seems clear that in view of the generous terms offered by Bagnall, the decision to accept at least one locomotive from that firm had been made. After November 1897 no more was heard from any other locomotive builder. The first locomotive to arrive at the quarry, the Bagnall-built CLIFFE, was already at work, having been delivered in November 1896, and another Bagnall, ISABEL, arrived in January 1897. The first locomotive, intended for the "main line", as opposed to those designed for work in the quarry itself, was delivered in August 1898 and named THE ROCKET. Mr Bagnall's firm had also quoted for the supply of both wooden and steel side-tipping wagons and many were in fact bought, together with some from other firms.

Whilst negotiating for the supply of locomotives, wagons and other equipment, agreement over trans-shipment facilities had been concluded with the Midland Railway. Work commenced on 16 September 1896 without the junketing associated with such events on public railways (although it is hard to believe that a few toasts at least were not drunk by the Quarry Co. Directors and the contractors). The line was quite a difficult one to build and was not ready for traffic until May 1897, the loads meanwhile being taken by the struggling traction engines which were finding the traffic more and more overwhelming. When they were displaced they continued to work however, but in more humble capacities, for instance hauling portable boilers used for supplying steam for drills. The McLaren engine was fitted with a different kind of exhaust pipe whilst employed on this job and as so altered the steam came up a separate pipe placed behind the chimney to prevent water dripping into the smokebox. This engine lasted until 1914 but the fate of the other one is not recorded.

The various sources of information that have been consulted refer to Bagworth Station as being the loading point for the traffic before the railway was built, but this seems rather odd for the following reasons. The route to Bagworth by road was very undulating, whereas to the sidings at Beveridge Lane it was mainly downhill or level and would have not been any greater distance. Almost conclusive is the reference to "Cliffhill Sidings" shown in the usual place but without any

THE ROCKET on embankment construction duty in 1911. Collection: Andrew Neale.

Rural scene. JACK (the second) heads a train of skip wagons along the "main line" of the Cliffe Hill Granite Co.
Collection: Andrew Neale.

Tramway, as shown on the 25in scale map of 1880. It is also shown thus on the 6in scale maps of 1884 and 1885, and it seems clear that most of the stone did in fact go to this point, first of all by horse and cart and later by traction engine.

There is an intriguing reference in the immortal book "Minimum Gauge Railways" by Sir Arthur Percival Heywood (1898), to a quarry owner of his acquaintance who used traction engines to haul a total of 30,000 tons of stone per year for 2½ miles over appalling roads and had to pay the local authorities £400 per annum for each engine in taxation. This was in spite of the fact that they (the local authorities) were either incapable or unwilling to keep the roads in decent repair, and had refused to allow him to build a light railway because of the large number of level crossings involved. This poses the question as to whether the quarry referred to was the Cliffe Hill or its predecessor – the mileage quoted would be about right and the company certainly used traction engines, but the figure of 30,000 tons a year seems very high for the period in question. It is an interesting speculation to say the least!

CHAPTER THREE
UP HILL
AND DOWN DALE

ALTHOUGH THE "MAIN LINE" of the Cliffe Hill Granite Co. changed very little during its life, the same cannot be said of the tracks in the Quarry. Unfortunately neither author saw the quarry lines first hand; Maurice Billington did not visit until 1950 by which time nearly all the track had been lifted, and David Smith was not even born! The description has of necessity to be based on the 1929 O.S. map with one or two supplementary notes related by former employees.

In the quarry, the two long branches from "Bluebell" and "Joskin" (unfortunately the origin of the names is clouded in mystery) climbed steeply from their respective faces and joined at a point

The railway passes Newlands Farm, owned by Breeden Everard; the passing loop is to the right. c.1900.
Collection: Maurice Billington.

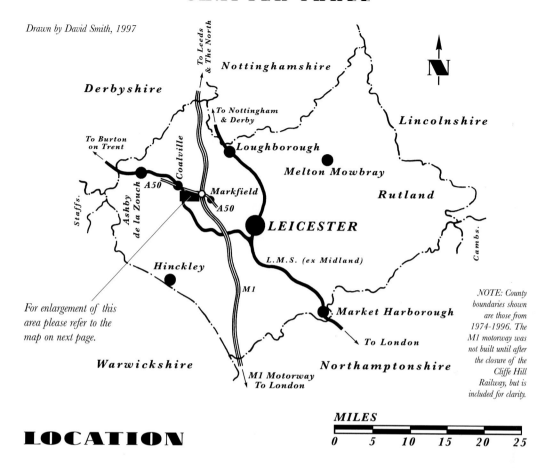

Drawn by David Smith, 1997

To Leeds & The North

Nottinghamshire

N

Derbyshire

To Nottingham & Derby

Lincolnshire

To Burton on Trent

Coalville

Loughborough

Staffs.

Ashby de la Zouch

A50

Markfield

A50

Melton Mowbray

Rutland

LEICESTER

Cambs.

Hinckley

L.M.S. (ex Midland)

M1

For enlargement of this area please refer to the map on next page.

Market Harborough

To London

NOTE: County boundaries shown are those from 1974-1996. The M1 motorway was not built until after the closure of the Cliffe Hill Railway, but is included for clarity.

Warwickshire

M1 Motorway To London

Northamptonshire

MILES

| 0 | 5 | 10 | 15 | 20 | 25 |

LOCATION

near to the crusher. Branches left this line to go to the hoppers, and the sett and kerb dressing sheds. Another line crossed high over the road on a girder bridge to the spoil bank whilst the tracks proceeded past the large hoppers before leaving the quarry area.

The "Main Line" or "Tramway" left the quarry area through a gate giving access to the road, which it crossed at an obtuse angle to take up its position on the left hand side. From this point, the tramway, at a slightly lower level than the road from which it was separated by a hedge, climbed steadily for about 350 yards to the point where it crossed the road, protected by gates, which climbed up from Stanton-Under-Bardon village.

The original route of the tramway continued on the same side of the road, but behind a low wall, down the dip and at the bottom passed through a gate and crossed Billa Barra Road near where it joined the Stanton road, which continues towards "The Flying Horse" public house on the main Leicester-Coalville road, and on to Copt Oak and Loughborough. (Now the B591.)

In crossing Billa Barra Road, the line turned very sharply and commenced to climb alongside the road, from which it was now separated by a hedge, the climb was quite short but steep initially, then it eased and for another 200 yards or so climbed to the summit and then descended for a similar distance to the point where Billa Barra Road was again crossed.

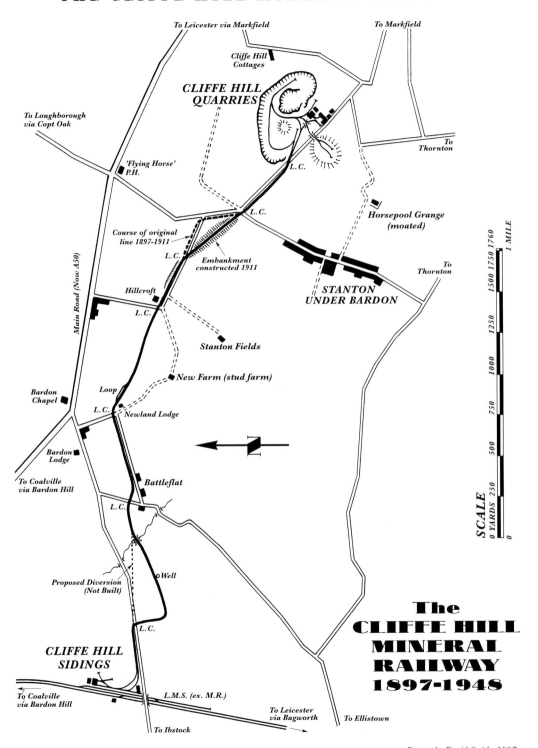

To Leicester via Markfield

To Markfield

Cliffe Hill Cottages

CLIFFE HILL QUARRIES

To Loughborough via Copt Oak

To Thornton

'Flying Horse' P.H.

L.C.

Horsepool Grange (moated)

L.C.

Course of original line 1897-1911

L.C.

Embankment constructed 1911

To Thornton

Hillcroft

STANTON UNDER BARDON

L.C.

Main Road (Now A50)

Stanton Fields

New Farm (stud farm)

Bardon Chapel

Loop

L.C.

Newland Lodge

Bardon Lodge

To Coalville via Bardon Hill

Battleflat

L.C.

Proposed Diversion (Not Built)

Well

L.C.

CLIFFE HILL SIDINGS

L.M.S. (ex. M.R.)

To Coalville via Bardon Hill

To Leicester via Bagworth

To Ellistown

To Ibstock

SCALE

0 YARDS 250 500 750 1000 1250 1500 1750 1760

0 1 MILE

The CLIFFE HILL MINERAL RAILWAY 1897-1948

Drawn by David Smith, 1997

MARY on a train of skips comes off the embankment, and is about to cross Billa Barra Lane.
Collection: David H. Smith.

This combination of a dip, a sharp curve and then a climb made operation of the old route very difficult and in fact locomotives and wagons were derailed on more than one occasion, whilst the grade precluded more than 10 full wagons being hauled. In 1911 a diversion was built, starting at the Stanton road, passing along a 350 yard embankment, before crossing Billa Barra Road at an obtuse angle and re-joining the original route, but at a different level. Advantage was taken at the time of constructing the embankment to level off the remainder of the bank and a cutting was made, in parts as much as 10 feet deep.

Near the second crossing of Billa Barra Road, the lovely house "Hillcroft" was built for Peter Lionel Preston in the early 1920's after a great deal of difficulty in boring for water.

It was the practice once the train had cleared the road crossing (which again was gated) to place "slippers" (or scotch blocks) under the wheels, one pair to each third wagon, to assist in braking the loaded train down the steep slope of Billa Barra Hill to the 24 wagon long loop at the bottom, some 600 yards away.

The scenery on this section was really fine, with views over open country on the left towards the stud farm known as Newland Farm and owned by Breedon Everard, and beyond towards the hills. To the right of the line the view was also delightful, looking towards the main Leicester-Coalville road and the hills and woods of Charnwood Forest.

After the loop the line curved to the left and under some overhanging trees just by Newland Lodge (sometimes called "Bancrofts Lodge" after the people who lived there). Originally the line had been laid with hardly any earth works, but the ground by the lodge was far from level and over the course of the years it was made up, the first time being in late 1897 which would account for the gradient of the incline having eased from 1 in 20 to 1 in 49. It was made up again during the early thirties and at about the same time the opportunity was taken to supplement the main loop with a smaller one to take twelve wagons situated across the minor road just beyond the Lodge. This road was not gated and was the scene of the motor cycle accident referred to later, the small loop was on the site of a very much earlier one, probably the original loop, which must have been replaced almost as soon as it was built.

The tramway then ran behind the hedge, alongside the road and climbed very slightly on a low embankment and on this section a brick trough was provided for the cattle in Mr Neal's field, just across the road from the southern part of Battleflat hamlet. It seems that his pond had to be passed where the line curved to cross the next road, and this prevented his cattle from drinking there so the company had to provide the trough and fill it with water every day. It was said that on the (fortunately rare) occasions when the tank wagon was omitted from the rake of the first train, the poor cattle would stand there by the trough waiting for their precious water and when it did finally arrive the engine men would have to prevent them from drinking to excess by the use of shovels on their rumps. At times they could be seen actually swelling as they drank!

Skirting Neal's pond the line then crossed the road from Ellistown, again through gates and it then ran at the back of Mr Neal's farm and continued for another 200 yards to a ditch which was crossed by a small cast iron bridge, the line was still on a slight embankment and in another 180 yards the well was reached. This was deep and in the very early days water had to be pumped by hand. This was a laborious business and very soon a Tangye steam pump, powered by a vertical boiler which was said to operate at 10 lbs per square inch pressure, was provided. The pump had a 3in delivery pipe and the tank could be filled in a few minutes. There was also a small sand drying attachment to the boiler and the whole place was looked after by an old man who lived nearby. In the course of time the boiler wore out and again hand pumping had to be reverted to, but by this time a younger man had taken over.

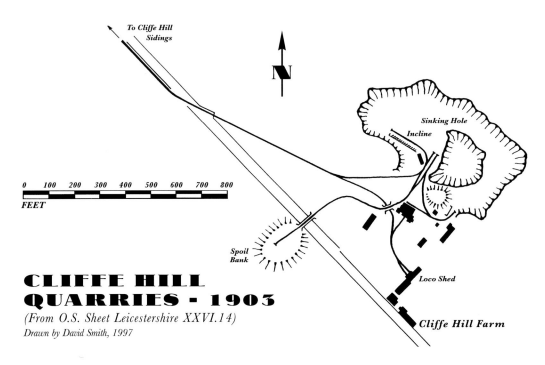

To Cliffe Hill
Sidings

N

Sinking Hole

Incline

0   100   200   300   400   500   600   700   800

FEET

Spoil
Bank

Loco Shed

CLIFFE HILL
QUARRIES - 1903
(From O.S. Sheet Leicestershire XXVI.14)
Drawn by David Smith, 1997

Cliffe Hill Farm

During the times of water shortage at the quarry, locomotives had to travel to the well for boiler washing out purposes, and then raise sufficient steam to travel back to the quarry. MARY was fairly quick at this, but JACK was for some reason rather slower; the usual method was to affix a large wad of cotton waste to a wire, soak this in paraffin and then set it on fire and run it around inside the firebox to help the combustion when the fire was laid. When there was a plentiful supply of water at the quarry this practice of washing out the locomotives at the well ceased.

It was barely another 300 yards from the well to "Neal's Curve" where the line described virtually a 90° turn of 60 feet radius to the right and continued for another 200 yards to the Beveridge Lane crossing which it approached between trees and hedges. The road was of course protected by gates but the crossing was on a curve. The line then disappeared behind a tall hedge, emerging to cross the lane up to Canister Farm in about 30 yards. It again went behind the hedge for the final stretch of a quarter mile to the sidings, a most attractive but difficult section. Had the 1915 cut-off (to be described in Chapter 5) materialised in accordance with McCarthy's plan the line would have left the existing route some 140 yards from Neal's Farm and would have taken a straight line right up to the road crossing, only a quarter mile in length. The road crossing, had it been constructed exactly as shown on the plan, would have been 140 yards in length instead of the 60 feet or so which it actually was. Another water supply would have been needed as the well would have been by-passed.

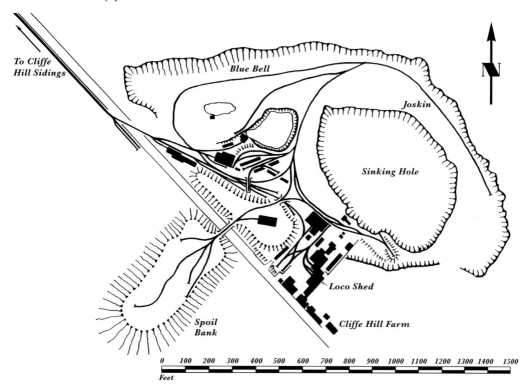

CLIFFE HILL QUARRIES - 1929

(From O.S. Sheet Leicestershire XXVI.14)

Drawn by David Smith, 1997

Incidentally, part of the land which the company leased in the region of Billa Barra Hill was from the Bardon Estate and was rented from a Mr Assheton Penn Curzon-Howe Herrick of Clifton Castle, Ripon, Yorkshire.

A reference to MARY in the "Locomotive Magazine" dated October 1912, stated that the line was approximately 3 miles long with gradients of 1 in 34 with the load, and 1 in 22 to empty trains, but it is hard to reconcile this with the information given earlier in Hunslet's letter. It also states that the line was originally laid with 24 lb per yard rails but was in the course of being relaid with 40 lb per yard. It would seem that at a later date, to counteract the tendency to spread on the curves (of which there were many!) cast iron chairs were added, rather than just rely on the usual practice of being spiked direct to the sleepers. Journey times were approximately 15 minutes from the quarry to the sidings, and a total of 1 hour was allowed, to include time for shunting at each end of the line. The average day's work for the locomotive was 6 return journeys each day, fuel consumption being 9 cwts of coal and 620 gallons of water.

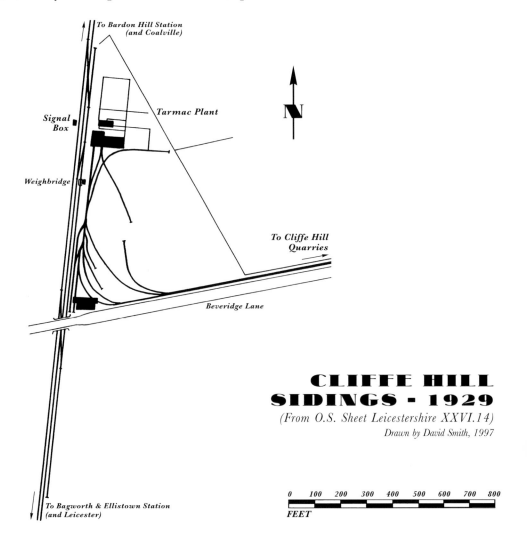

**CLIFFE HILL
SIDINGS - 1929**
(From O.S. Sheet Leicestershire XXVI.14)
Drawn by David Smith, 1997

CHAPTER FOUR
PROGRESS AND EXPANSION

BY 1900 OUTPUT WAS INCREASING rapidly, and the storage of waste was becoming a problem. It was decided to build a high level bridge crossing the road to link the quarry plant with a new waste tip. The bridge of girder construction was a very fine piece of engineering and in September 1901 one of the old traction engines was used to haul the first top girder into position, the bridge being completed shortly afterwards. The third quarry locomotive, EDITH, had arrived in May 1900, and in 1901 another main line locomotive, JACK, was bought and this fleet sufficed for another ten years. Also around this time the second level of the quarry - the "Sinking Hole" – was started, and it expanded rapidly. At first the stone was loaded into pans and these would be swung out of the hole by a three ton movable crane; two pans would fill a tub wagon in a train standing on the first level, and when all the tubs were filled the locomotive would haul the train to the mill for crushing, or alternatively go to the sett making or kerb dressing sheds.

With the increasing production of crushed stone came the problem of disposing of the coarse dust which could not be sold, so the Directors decided to erect a paving slab press near the Railway sidings. A press was bought from Fielding & Platt of Gloucester and commenced production in 1903. The venture was a great success and in the course of a year or two a concrete

JACK (second) about to cross Billa Barra Lane next to "Hillcroft" heading towards Beveridge Lane.
Collection: Maurice Billington.

block-making machine was also erected close by. These were followed by other buildings for use as workshops, stores and an office. Thus, the making of slabs and blocks became an important part of the Company's activities.

It was only natural that when the Company held its Annual General Meeting at the quarry that the Directors would wish to inspect the plant at the sidings. Motor cars were hardly known in those days, so the V.I.P.s had to travel there by rail and a special coach was provided for their conveyance; it had four wheels and was approximately ten feet in length and had a central partition with seats on each side so that eight people could use it, sitting four per side, back to back and looking outwards over the pretty countryside. There was no glass but the coach did have ends and may have had a canopy, but alas no drawings or photographs are known to exist and opinions differ on this point. In any event it must have been a very pleasant trip when the sun was shining, though it is doubtful if the coach was used if the weather was inclement!

In 1904 the Company bought its first batch of standard gauge wagons of twenty ton capacity, these were painted red with the words "Cliffe Hill Stone Pavement" in white diagonally along the sides. Eventually a total of 160 of these wagons were in use plus two special cement vans, and they travelled all over the country carrying the Company's products and of course publicising them.

By 1911 the severe curvature of the line, particularly at the crossing of Billa Barra Lane, was preventing the most efficient use of the locomotives. So it was decided that in spite of the expense involved an embankment should be made from a point just beyond the Stanton Lane crossing, to

Paving slabs being loaded into Midland Railway wagons at Cliffe Hill Sidings.
The slabs were marked "Cliffe Hill Stone", in this posed publicity photograph at least! Collection: Cliffe Hill Co.

A posed line-up of all the Company's locomotives c.1911. From right to left: EDITH (first), CLIFFE,
THE ROCKET, ISABEL, JACK (first), and MARY.
Collection: Andrew Neale.

a point only about 100 yards short of the summit of the line, to obviate the nasty crossing followed by the steep climb. Men came from Yorkshire, Wales and Ireland to supplement the local labour force and work was carried on by the aid of floodlights at night. Locomotives were used at both ends of the embankment for pushing the tubs of waste stone, but of course main line trains took precedence and those engaged on embankment work had to run on to the embankment when a train from either the quarry or the sidings wished to pass. This sustained effort from Easter to Christmas was rewarded however, by a superb embankment which contributed a great deal to the efficient running of the trains.

In the same year there came to the quarry the smartest little locomotive to be owned by the Company. Named MARY, it became the "pride of the line", and was lovingly cared for by drivers, fitters and all who were responsible. A new locomotive shed was even provided for MARY and "brother" locomotive JACK, which arrived three years later.

The year 1911 also witnessed the activities of a film company who came to the quarry. In those days of course, the art of motion pictures was in its infancy and would probably appear very crude to us today, but few enthusiasts could fail to be interested in the showing of this film if it were possible to see it. Unfortunately no record exists of who made it, let alone if it is still in existence.

In the following year 1912, a subsidiary company was formed to crush and market the brown skinned stone, which was in no way inferior to the grey stone but had hitherto been left unsold on account of its appearance. It was considered however, that after twenty years of marketing only grey stone that perhaps it would not be advisable to sell it under the Cliffe Hill name. To preserve the "image" of the Company it would be sold as "Rockside Stone", and a company known as "The Rockside Stone Company" was formed. Two jaw crushers and screens were housed in a building at the Stanton end of the quarry, the plant was driven by one of the old traction engines and the products had a ready sale. Even the dust was sold as it was found to be ideal for the making of tennis courts when mixed with rotten stone (known as "Gingerbread"), and this too enjoyed a good sale for many years.

CHAPTER FIVE
THE WAR YEARS
1914-1918

*Staff 1913 – Left to right, seated: P. L. Preston, P. Preston, J. R. Fitzmaurice (Company founder), T. Beedle and W. Shaw.
Standing: T. Swain, F. Gibson, H. J. Harwood, T. G. Hammond and A. E. Warner.*

IN 1913 NEW OFFICES were erected which were a vast improvement on the original ones and quite naturally the reconstituted stone used in the building was cast at the concrete works. The same year Peter Lionel Preston, son of the Manager, joined the Company after having served his apprenticeship with a Leicester firm of engineers, and he became Assistant Manager. One of his first tasks was to supervise the erection of a tar macadam plant at the sidings, this plant was constructed by Ord & Maddison of Darlington and was capable of a daily output of 200 tons of this very popular and sound product.

Deliveries of this material by road transport was preferred, direct to sites, and so the Company had no alternative but to enter into the road haulage business, and in 1914 purchased a Steam lorry built by Thomas Mann & Sons of Leeds. The carrying capacity was five tons but its speed was only 5 mph which therefore, limited its use to short journeys, but this new form of transport had its advantages and in 1915 a similar lorry was bought. Thus was the nucleus formed of a large and highly efficient road transport department.

As has been mentioned earlier a new locomotive, JACK, was bought in 1914, this was to replace the original locomotive of this name which was sold in 1916. The new locomotive was almost identical to MARY.

Another notable event which took place in 1914 was the use of the railway as a testing track for a petrol locomotive intended for use in India by the firm of Baguley Cars Ltd. of Burton-on-Trent. More details will be found in Chapter Nine.

The production of dressed materials reached its peak in 1914 but the coming of the First World War, "The war to end all wars", robbed the Company of a large number of younger men who volunteered to fight for their country. By the end of the war most of the older men were due for retirement and recruits to take their place were not forthcoming, no doubt owing to the arduous nature of the work and so started a decline in the stone dressing industry from which it never recovered. Within 5 years the output dropped by 60%, and by the time of the Second World War the trade was non-existent. With the passing of the stone dresser went one of the queerest customs in the quarrying industry. The stone dresser apparently regarded himself as "the elite" of quarrymen, he started his shift 5 minutes after the other men and gained another 5 minutes at the end of his shift, took his meals in a separate part of the mess room, took a break for elevenses in mid-morning, and when away from the job did not usually frequent the saloon or bar as did the other quarrymen.

In 1915 the Company prepared plans and estimates for a short "cut off" line to obviate the almost 90° bend near to the Beveridge Lane sidings, and had this been carried out, no doubt the improvement would have resulted in the line being worked to something like maximum efficiency,

A general view at Beveridge Lane. Note the standard gauge wagons in the foreground, and the gantry carrying buckets for discharge in those wagons. MARY and a train of skips can be seen in the background.
Collection: Maurice Billington.

but alas no records exist to show just why the plan was not proceeded with. Opposition from Lord Charnwood who was one of the principal landowners was mentioned to the writer, but he was also the owner of a very large number of Cliffe Hill shares and his opposition seems strange in view of this. Suffice it to say that the line was not built and the tramway had to continue its meandering course until the end.

During World War One another Mann steam lorry had arrived, second-hand this time, and as the road transport of products was gaining in popularity it was decided to increase the number of lorries. An Allchin articulated lorry, capable of a speed of 8 mph and carrying a load of 10 tons was ordered. This ran on solid rubber tyres instead of the steel plated wheels of the earlier ones, and so satisfied were the Company with this that they soon bought another from the same makers. A garage to house them was built by the roadside just below the quarry offices, a weighbridge for 20 tons and a weigh house was also built inside the quarry premises and a Weighbridgeman and his clerk also engaged. Hitherto the office staff in general had been responsible for the weighing of the carts and lorries.

Also by this time the "Sinking Hole" had expanded to a great extent, no longer were the pans being lifted out by the crane. A light 2 feet gauge track had been laid on the floor of the quarry on which the tubs were pushed by hand to a point where they were hauled out by a Parker Derrick crane. Before very long locomotives were in use on the quarry bottom, EDITH being the first to work down there shortly after the war had ended. The next step was to build an incline from the bottom of the "Sinking Hole" to the top of the quarry and this was done in 1920. The line came out at the Markfield ("Joskin") end of the hole and the tubs were hauled out two at a time by a steam winch housed in a small building on the top level. The drum for the wire rope was on a tower which was specially built for this purpose and it soon earned the name "The Monument", being seen clearly on the skyline in Markfield village over a mile away. It was the practice in later years to bring the locomotives out from the hole both at meal and at blasting times, and these were hauled out via the same method.

Standard gauge wagons being hauled out of the "Sinking Hole". Nearly obscured by the wagons waiting at the bottom is either SOUTHSEA or LORD MAYOR. Collection: Maurice Billington.

CHAPTER SIX
THE
ROARING TWENTIES

The main road entrance to the quarry c.1925 with many of the Company's road steam fleet awaiting duty.
Locomotive MARY is shunting a train of wagons.
Cliffe Hill Granite Co. "Official" – Collection: Maurice Billington.

BY THE EARLY 1920s the demand for setts and kerbs had declined considerably but to balance this, granite chippings were very popular and the Company improved its plant and methods in order to cope with the ever increasing demand for this product. Advantage was taken of the availability of almost-new locomotives following war service. MABEL was bought in March 1920, and this was followed in August 1922 by PETER, named after the Manager. In 1924 the steam engine at the Tarmacadam plant was dispensed with and the machinery converted to run off electric power. At the quarry itself the machinery had at first been powered by a De Dion petrol engine, this had been superseded by a Packard engine but this was also replaced when electric power became available. In 1924 too, Peter Preston retired as Manager and Secretary, but he accepted a seat on the Board of Directors and his son, Peter Lionel Preston, succeeded to his father's job.

The demand for the specially washed aggregate continued to grow and a quicker method of washing was sought. A large perforated drum was erected on a wooden structure, and turned on rotating rollers, water being fed to the drum as the aggregate passed through. The output of the product was doubled by this new method and the quality remained unimpaired.

In 1926 the Company secured its longest contract to date, the supply of approximately 30,000 tons of filter media to the Leicester Corporation Sewage Works at Beaumont Leys. The whole of this material was washed prior to delivery and the contract was completed to the customer's schedule within 18 months. To help with the delivery of this contract the Company purchased two Daimler six ton lorries mounted on solid rubber tyres (later modified to the pneumatic type). This new type of vehicle was certainly faster than the steam lorries but owing to the heavier costs of operation at that time there was no financial gain.

The days of the steam lorries were by no means over however, and they continued to deliver stone over a wide area, Long Eaton, Peterborough (on which route the steam lorries would be "breathless" by the time they had climbed Wardley Hill, near Uppingham) and for six months they were engaged in delivering loads of chippings for making concrete to Stoke-on-Trent for use in the building of a large Rubber Factory, presumably the Michelin plant. There were a number of differences between the various makes of steam lorry, the Mann's used to blow off into the chimney, but the Allchin's had a separate pipe behind the chimney, one of these latter machines had a Sunbeam lighting set somehow worked by steam from the boiler but all the others had Acetylene lamps. At this time there were no fewer than five lorries built by the Northampton firm and the three old Mann's were still active.

The year 1926 was a bad one for this country, which was bedevilled by labour disputes, strikes, lockouts and many other manifestations of dissatisfaction. During the coal strike which lasted for six weeks the Company was unable to obtain fuel for the locomotives and lorries, and various substitutes had to be used; wood and rubbish of all kinds were tried and it was found that old tyres from the lorries made the best of a bad job. In order to free the tyres from the wheels the method was to stack the wheel rims complete with tyres on top of each other and then light a fire inside the rims, this would melt the bonding cement and the tyres came off quite easily, it was much more difficult to cut the tyres however, a machine hacksaw was tried but was not very successful and so the staff had the unenviable job of using their pocket knives for the purpose. The black smoke and the pungent smell of locomotives and lorries using rubber as fuel must have been decidedly unpleasant, so doubtless when the strike was over and coal once more available all grades of quarry workers were profoundly thankful. Unfortunately this strike was followed by the General Strike with all its chaos and the real fear of rebellion. As a precaution, Police had to be engaged to guard the powder magazine.

As the work of the maintenance staff increased, their accommodation began to present difficulties and two large, airy shops were erected in the quarry yard. Smiths and millwrights occupied one, and carpenters and other maintenance men the other. A Sullivan drill sharpener was bought and this was a very useful addition as previously all the drills had been sharpened by hand.

In 1927 at the request of a Belgian firm of drillers a new method of drilling was tried out. A weighted drill was hoisted and dropped on to the rock, but this method proved much too slow in the tough granite. Modifications were made by the drillers from time to time and after a period of 18 months, four holes 6in in diameter and 20 feet deep were drilled. These were exploded in October 1928 and resulted in a fall of several thousand tons but it was badly fragmented and it

Cliff Hill Sidings signal box (the plate on which missed off the "e" from Cliff) can be seen in the background of this view of couple of labourers and three of the early pattern tipping wagons. Note the different wheelsets on the central wagon.
Collection: Andrew Neale.

needed a tremendous amount of secondary drilling during the next 18 months in order to clear the fall, and the Management were left quite unconvinced by the experiment! The year 1927 also saw a new type of locomotive arrive at the quarry, this time supplied by the Sentinel Company of Shrewsbury.

The following year a new 30in gyratory crusher was bought from Allis Chalmers, U.S.A., and when this was working fully it could crush much larger stones, weighing in fact up to a ton and so "knocking up to size" by hammers was no longer needed. A 10in secondary crusher was also bought from the same firm. Now that the new crushers were working and the operation speeded up considerably it was found that the only real flaw in the procedure was the rather slow method by which the loaded tubs were hauled out of the quarry. Two Smith's "Orange Peel" grab cranes were bought in order to speed the loading of the tubs and these were mounted on caterpillar tracks (Rail borne cranes of various types had been in use since about 1910). Even with these useful machines the time taken was felt to be too slow and so a completely new method (or rather a development of an old one) was inaugurated, but this involved the abandonment of the narrow gauge lines in the "Sinking Hole".

A superb general view of the quarry c.1925, with no less than five of the narrow gauge steam locomotives visible.
From left to right: ISABEL; centre distance PETER; loco on curved track is unknown;
THE ROCKET with 3 skip wagons; and MABEL (?) near the end of the small bridge.

Cliffe Hill Granite Co. "Official"; Collection: Maurice Billington.

CHAPTER SEVEN
THE THIRTIES

A general view of SOUTHSEA being loaded by an excavator in the "Sinking Hole".
Collection: Maurice Billington.

THE NEW WORKING METHOD described at the end of Chapter Six recalled the one used in the earliest days in the "Sinking Hole" in which pans of loaded stone had been brought out of the hole. But instead of small wooden pans the new ones were of steel construction and had a carrying capacity of 10 tons, the derrick which had been used in the early days was still in situ and well able to cope with these loads. It was also felt that as by this time some of the steam lorries were past their best years and not really suitable for work on the roads, that they could quite easily be used on the quarry floor, carrying loads to a point where the pan was waiting to receive them. The track was duly taken out in the late twenties and the lorries were lowered into the hole with the aid of the derrick. This method was certainly a great deal quicker than had been the case hitherto, but the very uneven floor, abounding in potholes was far from ideal for the lorries and they were constantly having to be lifted out of the hole to go for much needed repairs. The fitting gang had plenty of work in the form of replacing broken springs and axles, welding cracked chassis frames and the like. An idea considered by Peter L. Preston was to remove the water tanks from the lorries and fill up their boilers instead from a water stand pipe but it was not proceeded with. The old lorries soon wore out as a result of this rough usage, but they were replaced by others of later design. Cheaper second-hand machines were more easily available after the Road and Rail Traffic Act of 1933 passed into law.

Prior to 1933 the taxation system for steam or motor lorries was the same, £60 for any lorry, either four or six wheeled. With the passing of the act, tax was levied on unladen weight, but a maximum laden axle weight of 5 tons was imposed. Steamers were heavier unladen, and consequently, a smaller payload could be carried. Tax for steam lorries increased to £140 for a four wheeler, and £260 for a six wheeler and these rates were very much higher than they were for equivalent motor vehicles. Whatever the official reasons advanced for these impositions, it seems clear that the Government were determined to be rid of steam lorries on the roads. Motorists had been complaining for years about the poor visibility created by condensing steam in damp weather, but the manufacturers were not given the chance to improve the machines to obviate this and these penal rates of taxation had the desired objective. In spite of the grand work done by firms such as Sentinel and Foden to improve their machines, the days of the steam lorry were definitely numbered, and production had to be switched to the motor lorry even though, at that time, they were by no means as efficient as the steam lorries they replaced.

Faced with these impositions, the Company had no alternative but to buy more petrol lorries and the steamers, including two fine Allchins of 1929, were relegated to work in the hole where, for two or three years further, the lorries bumped and swayed over the uneven floor of the quarry. In wet weather their fires were almost doused by the water from deep pot holes and ruts, the continual weight of stone being dropped into them caused the bodies to break and the maintenance men fought a continuous battle against the deterioration brought about by rough usage. Two Maudsley petrol lorries joined the steamers for a short time but as can be imagined they were even more unsuited to this kind of treatment. So, however economical the method was in theory, the rapid deterioration of the lorries caused the Company to think again and the outcome of their deliberations was the decision to revert again to rail traction.

This time however, the Company took advantage of the second hand market for standard gauge locomotives, and in 1934 a Hunslet engine – SOUTHSEA – was bought, followed shortly after by a Hudswell Clark, of the same basic design of 0-4-0ST but incorporating of course the maker's traditional style. Two steel 10 ton wagons were constructed in the quarry workshops and in addition several wooden wagons of the same tonnage were bought after use on the construction of Birmingham Corporation's Elan Valley Water Board reservoirs at Rhayader, Radnorshire.

A new and much larger haulage gear was purchased and placed in an engine house at the top of the incline which was virtually the original, upon which 2 feet gauge tracks had been laid, but had been extended and widened to take standard gauge tracks. The original haulage house had been vacant for some years and had in fact been converted into a welding shop. The larger railway was a much more economical proposition as the winding engine could haul out three 10 ton wagons at a time and the crusher could now be used at something like its maximum efficiency, it also made Cliffe Hill one of the very small number of quarries having standard gauge track in the quarries but a narrow gauge main line, and having a very short length of mixed gauge track at the tipping dock for the mill.

Reverting back to 1933 however, the base of the new crusher cracked. A replacement could not be obtained other than from the U.S.A., and this involved the Company in a seven month wait. Fortunately the old jaw crushers had not been dismantled and in a few hours crushing was again possible, although the stone had first to be broken to a suitable size. It must have been a great day when the large crusher was back in commission.

In 1935 the Company purchased the freehold of the quarry and the surrounding property from the original founder, J. Rupert Fitzmaurice. The same year also saw another addition to the locomotive stock, this time narrow gauge and in the form of another Sentinel locomotive which was bought after use by the Durham County Water Board who had used it for the building of the large Burnhope reservoir. This engine bore no name when it arrived but was soon fitted with the nameplates off EDITH which was by that time redundant and only used for providing steam for rock drills etc.

A new Tarmacadam plant was erected at the quarry in 1937 suitable for bituminous chippings and the old Tar Plant at the sidings gave way to the new method and was dismantled, parts being incorporated in the new plant. The idea of Bitumen had been tried in the early 1930s when a small plant had been bought second hand, and its great success and popularity decided the Directors to invest in a much larger unit. More and larger motor lorries were bought in 1937 and the following year and a Ruston Bucyrus electric shovel was added to the stock of loading equipment. Holidays with pay were also inaugurated in the industry in 1939 and the Cliffe Hill employees were able to take a paid holiday in August of that year – unfortunately by that time the dark clouds of war had reappeared and it was to be the last happy holiday spent by many people, for very soon there were to be many trials and heartaches and things were never to be quite the same again.

MARY and KASHMIR at the passing loop near to Newland Lodge.
Why the locomotives have detached from their train is not clear, perhaps they are about to take water.
Collection: David H. Smith.

CHAPTER EIGHT
THE FINAL YEARS

Sentinel geared locomotive, EDITH (second) c.1945, showing the chain coupling between the driving wheels. The photograph also clearly shows details of the inside framed "V" skips.
Cliffe Hill Granite Co. "Official" – Collection: Maurice Billington.

THE WAR YEARS were extremely trying for the Company as they were for many thousands of individuals. It is true that in the early years there was an incessant demand for granite chippings and tarmacadam for use in airfield runways and for other materials used in the construction of munitions factories and the like, whilst the entire stock of matured paving slabs was bought by the Government for use in military camps. But the loss of the greater number of the young men to the forces, and the rationing of essential stores such as timber, tyres, springs, fuel and most of the other materials used in quarry maintenance made conditions very difficult and production was nothing like it had been immediately prior to the outbreak of war. It should be noted that (in summertime at any rate) the steam locomotives had been worked throughout the day and well into the evening, and powerful Acetylene headlights were used in darkness, but with the coming of the war and the danger of air raids this could not be continued and the fires had to be dropped at dusk. It was also decided to fit all over cabs to the locomotives in place of the bent weatherboards – a move which was heartily appreciated by the engine men who had, hitherto, braved the weather wrapped in oilskins. These improvements however were only applied to the "main line" locomotives.

Another locomotive came into stock in 1941 and this time was of a standard type of Kerr Stuart design which had seen much service in other places. Un-named at first it became KASHMIR in memory of Arnold Robinson, one of the Company's fitters who was lost whilst serving on the destroyer of that name which was sunk off Crete on 23rd May of that year. Peter Preston, the founder manager died in December 1942 after serving the Company for 51 years, 33 as Manager and 18 years on the Board of Directors.

In order to alleviate the chronic shortage of young men the Company obtained permission to employ a number of German and Italian prisoners of war. They were well disciplined and most of them worked well and were paid (or rather the War Office was paid) for their services at 1d per hour less than the normal quarry labourers rate. Their work was much appreciated and enabled the Company to continue production although on a reduced scale.

When the war ended in 1945 there was a tremendous leeway to make up. No new houses or roads had been built but many had been destroyed in air raids. As soon as National and local finances permitted, much needed reconstruction work was put in hand and in order to cope with the increased demand for materials. The Company had to erect an additional set of screens and a hopper to take the stone from the primary crusher which was working at its optimum, and with these additions it was possible to work on a double shift basis. Peter McHowell Preston, the son

The group of disused locomotives on the spoil bank on 8 October 1950. In the foreground are ISABEL and PETER, in the background (left to right): EDITH (second), THE ROCKET (with vertical Sentinel boiler in the cab), SAMSON/TUG, KASHMIR, MARY, and JACK (second). Late Ken Cooper – courtesy Industrial Railway Society.

The track is still in situ somewhere along the line in the mid 1950's.
Maurice Billington.

of the Managing Director, who had worked at the quarry before the war, returned from his service with the Royal Engineers and was appointed Quarry Manager, being the third generation of the family to serve in that capacity. One of his first tasks was to completely reorganise the haulage scheme in the quarry, and he decided to use five heavy American "Mack" lorries in place of the Standard Gauge locomotives in the "Sinking Hole". Once again the track was taken up, the incline abandoned and a road was made to enable the lorries, with a capacity of 12 tons, to convey the stone in a most economical manner to the crusher. With further quarrying extensions the course of the old incline was completely obliterated.

By 1947 the two long narrow gauge branches to "Bluebell" and "Joskin" were out of use and the locomotives did not have a great deal to do, being limited to shunting around the gravel mill, to and from the storage hoppers and work at the tarmac plant. A small diesel locomotive had been bought for this work but was none too reliable and a steam engine often had to do its work. The lorries had by this time proved their worth however, and by early 1948 the two feet gauge lines in the quarry were abandoned. Clearly the fate of the "main line" was in doubt, but Peter L. Preston was loth to see that abandoned altogether without having the line tested against the capacity of the lorries. His voice prevailed to the extent that the fitters were told to keep the locomotives in good order, whilst the lorries were being tried to assess their moving capacities, just in case they failed to measure up to his son's expectations. The right of way was maintained but it was almost

The course of the railway across the embankment is now used as a footpath.
View looking towards Beveridge Lane, 21 April 1984.
Maurice Billington.

a foregone conclusion that the lorries would win the battle and in March 1948 the railway to Beveridge Lane was used for the last time with many regrets, but the cold law of economics had dictated that the locomotives should be dispensed with and the lovely sight and sound of MARY or JACK blasting hard up the bank, bell ringing at the crossings, had gone for ever and instead just the roar of a petrol or diesel engine, clouds of dust in summer, muddy roads in winter were to be the scene from then on.

Fortunately the locomotives were not scrapped immediately, in fact only MABEL was cut up there and then as it had not worked for some time. The two Standard Gauge locomotives were soon sold, but the remaining stock was shunted across the girder bridge to a resting place on the spoil bank where they were to stay for another nine years. They were to be seen and photographed by many lovers of Industrial and Narrow Gauge locomotives. From time to time they were inspected by prospective buyers and it was even thought that the best ones might have been sold and have a new lease of life in India, but apparently some aspect of the boilers did not conform to Indian standards and so this interesting deal did not take place.

One locomotive, ISABEL, was sold to Messrs W. G. Bagnall in response to their request for an example for preservation of the type which had helped them to make their name for simplicity and robustness, and which quite naturally they were delighted to know was still working after 50 years. The locomotive was moved to Stafford in March 1953; the full story up to date is told in Chapter Twelve.

Great changes came over the quarry; large rear dumpers replaced the Mack lorries, new crushers were installed, linked together with screens and hoppers by conveyors and all the modern appurtenances of efficient quarrying, the hole had increased many times over the size of the original. Indeed a third level was started in 1962 and now little remains at the quarry to recall the days of the steam locomotives.

The original founder of the quarry, J. Rupert Fitzmaurice, died in September 1949 and his place taken by F. W. Grant. In that same year the Company embarked on a completely new product, that of ready mixed concrete, well known in the U.S.A. and on the Continent but hardly known here until then. A road vehicle was used with a specially designed body and local contractors were asked if they would give it a trial, they did and were highly delighted with the product and this has now become one of the main selling lines of the Company.

In 1954 Peter Lionel Preston, Chairman of the Board, died after serving the Company for

A section of spiked flat bottom track is exposed at Beveridge Lane 36 years after the last train ran; 21 April 1984.
Maurice Billington.

42 years. His son (Peter McHowell Preston) who had been appointed Joint Managing Director two years earlier, was now appointed Managing Director and L. C. Simpson elected to the Chairmanship of the Board.

The track on the railway lay in situ for several years and the route was used as an unofficial footpath, however most of it had been lifted by 1955 and the rest, from Battleflat crossing to the foot of the incline was lifted by local enthusiast John Vernon and a group of willing helpers in 1967. A railway was laid in the grounds of Church Farm, at Newbold Verdon, only some six miles from Cliffe Hill, but this was dismantled in the 1980s. Some of the track was then sold to the Amberley Museum in Sussex, and so a Cliffe Hill locomotive, PETER (see Chapter Eleven), now operates over Cliffe Hill track, albeit many miles from the original site.

The fine girder bridge over the road was dismantled in 1960, but the abutments remained for some years longer, though they vanished in the 1970s. Fortunately the most tangible evidence of the Railway, the 1911 embankment, still stands though it is a matter for conjecture just how long it will continue to do so in these days of high prices for farm (and all other) land. Whilst it does, it is still possible to picture a train hauled by MARY or JACK, with plenty of steam and smoke, with perhaps Joe Allen at the regulator, ringing the bell for the Stanton Lane crossing.

So ends the story of the Cliffe Hill Railway, and some of the men who worked on it. The quarry is still working today (early 1997), although since 1963 it has been part of the Tarmac Group, but the story of its modern achievements do not form part of "the railway era".

CHAPTER NINE
LOCOMOTIVES AND ROLLING STOCK

CLIFFE in the quarry on 21 June 1937. Late George Alliez – Collection: Allan C Baker.

CONSIDERING THAT THE VAST MAJORITY of the Company's locomotives were built by one firm, W. G. Bagnall Ltd. of Castle Engine Works in Stafford, the stock was of a varied selection, and fortunately it is possible to trace the history of most of them. A tabulated version of the locomotive history, together with a list of known dimensions can be found at the end of the Chapter.

CLIFFE

The first locomotive, named CLIFFE, was a standard design of Bagnall 0-4-0ST, with 6in x 9in outside cylinders and a circular steel firebox ("bull-head" type in Bagnall parlance). It was fitted with the "patent" valve gear, designed by E. E. Baguley, the makers' Chief Draughtsman, which had a high linkage and was thus very suitable for locomotives working in quarries where large pieces of stone, lying close to the track, could interfere with the action of, say, the better known Walschaerts gear. CLIFFE was the firm's No. 1487 and was constructed to a "stock order" dated

The former CLIFFE, seen in use at nearby Bardon Hill Quarry, c.1950.
Late Ken Cooper – Courtesy Industrial Railway Society.

5 March 1896. When Cliffe Hill required locomotives, Bagnall's were able to supply No. 1487 (and 1491, below) from stock, and it was dispatched from Stafford on 17 November 1896, at a cost of £325. It arrived at the quarry three days later on 20 November, the livery being dark green, and it was regarded as quite a good little engine. Bagnall supplied many spares for CLIFFE, including on 2 June 1899 the provision of a crosshead driven water pump to replace one of two injectors; the last recorded spares being ordered in 1932.

CLIFFE worked at the quarry until 1946 when it was sold to the neighbouring Bardon Hill Quarry of Messrs Ellis & Everard, and it finally vanished from there around 1953.

ISABEL

The second locomotive ordered at the same time was named ISABEL. It was a slightly larger 0–4–0ST with 7in x 12in cylinders, and thus slightly more powerful than CLIFFE. Ordered for stock on 14 May 1896, maker's number 1491 was dispatched from Stafford on 9 February 1897, at a cost of £385, and it too was popular with the crews, and had a long life at the quarry. Like CLIFFE it was fitted with a crosshead driven pump to replace an injector in 1899, but ISABEL's circular, marine type firebox evidently gave trouble, because Bagnall's supplied a boiler with a conventional locomotive type firebox in January 1898. The old boiler was returned to Bagnall, who rebuilt it with copper firebox and brass tubes (these were steel originally) and used as "new" in the construction of No. 1551, supplied in September 1899 to Fisher & LeFana Mourne in

Above: ISABEL looking rather the worse for wear (note the front buffer beam, the cylinder sheeting, and the patches on the cab sheets) on 21 June 1937. Late George Alliez – Collection: Allan C. Baker.

Below: The other side of ISABEL taken about the same time. Collection: Maurice Billington.

Ireland. New larger tubes were provided for ISABEL in 1905, and a replacement (conventional) firebox fitted to the boiler in September 1908. In February 1931, a new boiler, reverting to the circular type firebox was supplied by Bagnall. The last recorded new spares were ordered on 22 March 1932.

ISABEL was last used at Cliffe Hill in 1948, but in March 1953 she was acquired by her makers for preservation; the rest of the story will be related in Chapter 12.

THE ROCKET on 21 June 1937. Note the unusual saddle tank shape and equally unusual outer valance, almost a second frame. This, and JACK (first) were the only locos built to this design.
Late George Alliez – Collection: Allan C. Baker.

THE ROCKET

The first locomotive built expressly for service on the "main line" was ordered from Bagnall on 28 January 1898 and dispatched from Stafford on 6 August in the same year, at a cost of £485. This was THE ROCKET, bearing the makers' No. 1531 and was quite a different design to the previous locomotives (although it shared the same cylinder size as ISABEL), having an unusual semi-double frame arrangement, whereby the external valence was substantial enough to give the impression of having outside frames. It also had an equally unusual saddle tank, shaped to look like a cross between a conventional round saddle tank and Great Western Railway style pannier tanks. It had a locomotive type copper firebox, instead of the firm's well known circular type, presumably as a result of the experience with ISABEL. The livery was specified as "Midland Brown" and this may explain why this and other Cliffe Hill locomotives varied between chocolate and dark red, since the Midland Railway went through a period when it used a brown livery

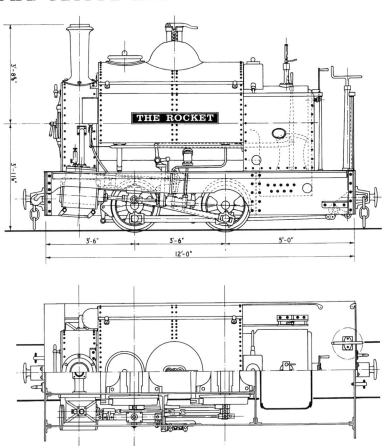

W. G. Bagnall Ltd. 0-4-0ST 'THE ROCKET'
Works No. 1531 - 1898

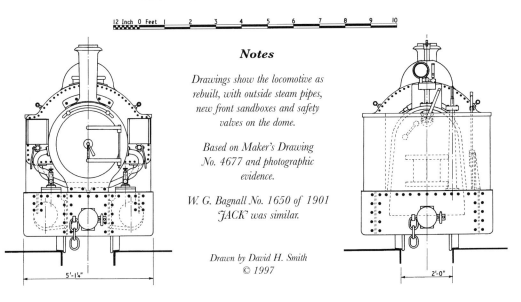

Notes

Drawings show the locomotive as rebuilt, with outside steam pipes, new front sandboxes and safety valves on the dome.

Based on Maker's Drawing No. 4677 and photographic evidence.

W. G. Bagnall No. 1650 of 1901 'JACK' was similar.

Drawn by David H. Smith
© 1997

rather than the better known rich deep red. Perhaps the Cliffe Hill company changed from brown to red when Midland did too. It was certainly not unknown elsewhere for industrial railway locomotive liveries to mirror the local main line company. The safety valves were originally placed over the firebox, but the engine men complained of the steam blowing into their faces so these were removed and placed instead in the top of the dome. Just when this alteration was carried out is not recorded but it was certainly before 1911 as a photograph showing THE ROCKET engaged on the embankment contract shows this clearly. On 30 July 1919, an order was placed with Bagnall for a new firehole door ring, and it is likely that this work was carried out in the course of other repairs at Stafford. In 1923 new "special crankpins" were supplied.

THE ROCKET worked hard for the Company, particularly on trips to and from the sidings before being replaced on this work by MARY, it was derailed on the old line at the sharp bend in Billa Barra Lane, but was not severely damaged. In 1927 it was run into by the new Sentinel locomotive at a spot called "The Nants" in the quarry, but never left the track, for a time it was fitted to use oil fuel but this was not a great success and coal was reverted to. However, by 1946 the locomotive was badly in need of a new boiler, but as the Company were at that time considering the abandonment of the 2ft-0in gauge lines it was felt that the cost of a normal boiler could not be entertained, so as an experiment THE ROCKET was fitted with a spare vertical boiler as used in a Sentinel lorry. This was fitted and the various modifications made by the very capable gang of fitters under the control of Fred Boulds but as he rightly suspected, it proved not to be a success. The engine as rebuilt would only work for a period of ten minutes or so, and would then have to "blow up" for a further twenty minutes in order to recover steam; it only worked for a very short time in this state before the boiler was removed and it was withdrawn and moved to the spoil bank. However it was not finally scrapped until 1957 when sold to Frank Berry of Leicester, along with all the remaining locomotives.

EDITH (1)

EDITH was the next locomotive, arriving in May 1900, and was identical to CLIFFE except for having 1ft 7in diameter wheels. This was Bagnall's No. 1589, ordered for stock on 20 October 1899, enabling the maker to fulfil Cliffe Hill's order dated 24 January 1900. No. 1589 was dispatched from Stafford on 8 May 1900 at a cost of £350, and painted Midland brown like THE ROCKET. Little is known of her exploits except that it was the first locomotive to work in the "Sinking Hole" in 1920 where it was later joined by CLIFFE which for some reason was the better engine. A new saddle tank was supplied in March 1921, but by 1934 EDITH had been withdrawn from normal work and was used instead for supplying steam for the rock drills, the nameplate was removed and fitted to the second Sentinel locomotive in 1935 but the date of the Bagnall's actual demise is not recorded.

JACK (1)

Another locomotive, virtually identical to THE ROCKET and also for use on the Tramway, was ordered on 15 February 1901 and dispatched on 8 July of the same year, just outside the specified 16 week period. This was makers' No. 1650, and was named JACK. Like THE ROCKET she was capable of hauling 14 wagons over the old course of the tramway but it was not as popular as the first locomotive of this type, perhaps because of a tendency to develop hot axleboxes; the rear overhang which was the same as THE ROCKET, gave more problems, and perhaps this explains the need for alterations to the buffer beams by Order dated February 1911. Despite the

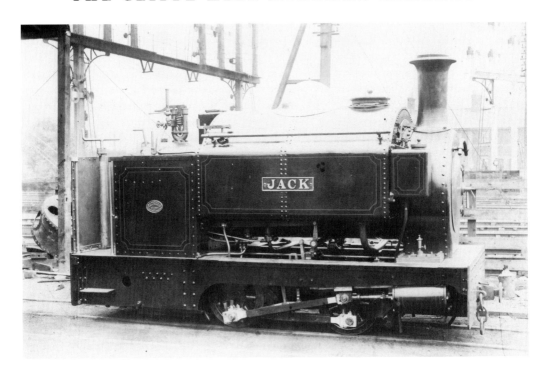

Above: The first JACK seen in the Bagnall works yard at Stafford prior to delivery to Cliffe Hill.
Collection: Allan C. Baker.

Below: The first JACK seen at the quarry c.1911. Soon afterwards, the second JACK was delivered and this loco was sold.
Collection: David H. Smith.

EDITH after being taken out of use on the railway, but still providing steam for rock drills and other quarry equipment. Late P. W. Robinson – Collection: Frank Jones.

problems a rather neat weatherboard was fitted to JACK in December 1910, but not to THE ROCKET.

When the second 0-4-2T was delivered for use on the main line in 1915, JACK was declared surplus to requirements, loosing its name to the newcomer. Interestingly, some spares were ordered on 12 February 1916, presumably with a view to selling the locomotive as a working machine; the purchaser being the Graham's Moor Quarries Co. Ltd. of Shrewsbury for use at their quarry at Breidon Hill at the end of the Criggion branch of the Shropshire & Montgomeryshire Light Railway. They had advertised in "Contract Journal" on 10 May 1916, "... wanted – small 2ft 4in gauge loco ...", but were ordering spares for Bagnall 1650 by 20 June, so transfer would presumably have taken place between those dates. So far as is known, the gauge of the loco was not altered (indeed it would have been difficult with the substantial outside valences), so perhaps the railway was altered to suit the locomotive. The name JACK seems to have been retained at Breidon Hill, but the narrow gauge there was replaced by road transport about 1930 and the locomotive scrapped.

MARY

The locomotive stock already described sufficed for another 10 years until a locomotive of quite a different type arrived for use on the tramway. This was MARY, Works No. 1943, which was ordered on 5 April 1911 and dispatched to Bardon Hill Station en route to Cliffe Hill Sidings on 1 July of that year, at a cost of £535. It was of a particularly pleasing design, an 0-4-2 side tank

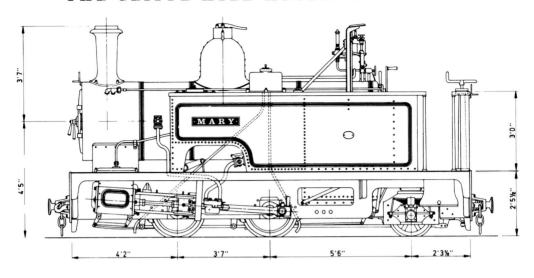

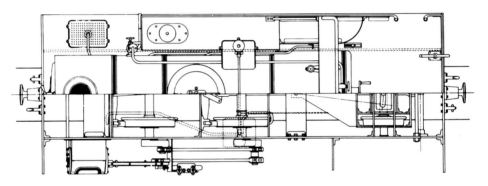

W. G. Bagnall Ltd. 0-4-2T 'MARY'
Works No. 1943 - 1911

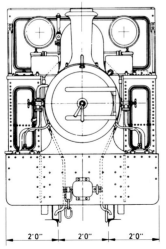

Notes

*Based on maker's pipe arrangement
drawing and photographic evidence.*

*Wheel bearings and springs
omitted from plan.*

*Works No. 2034, JACK of 1914,
was similar, but not identical.*

Drawn by E. A. Wade, © 1973

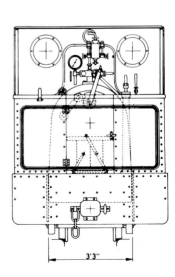

Above and below: Manufacturers photographs of MARY, resplendent in its chocolate brown paint, lined yellow and black, taken at Stafford. Bagnall's were clearly pleased with the locomotive because they photographed it twice (!), and it became the flagship of the Cliffe Hill fleet. Collection: Allan C. Baker.

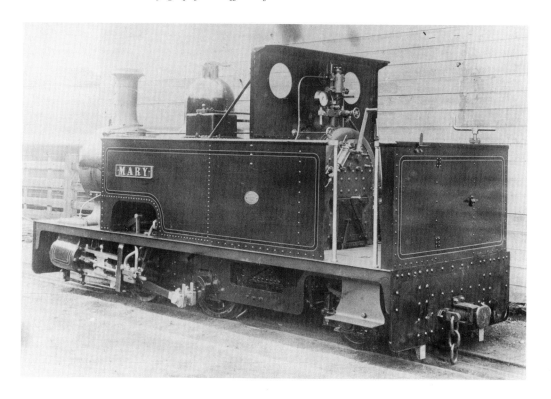

MARY on 21 June 1937, still very little altered from as-built condition. The driver is Joe Allan.
Late George Alliez – Collection: Allan C. Baker.

with larger cylinders and wheels than anything preceding it, and it was delivered complete with weatherboard. The livery was specified as "…same as Midland Railway locomotives…" and it would seem that MARY was originally painted chocolate, lined out yellow and black, but was later re-painted dark red. (See under THE ROCKET for a possible explanation of the change of livery). Originally fitted with a standard type of whistle, this was replaced with a neat bell cast by the local firm of bell founders, George Taylor & Co. of Loughborough. Acetylene headlights which at one time had been fitted to the steam lorries were also fitted at about this time and these gave a much improved light compared with the old Colza oil lamps. MARY would take 18 loaded wagons easily and on more than one occasion, hauled the maximum of 24 wagons, and in view of this greater, more economical length of train, the loop at Battleflat had to be lengthened to suit.

Unlike all the locomotives so far described (which were fitted with Baguley "Patent" valve gear), MARY was fitted with "Bagnall-Price" gear which had to be developed to replace the earlier type, following Baguley's severance with Bagnall. The works manager, S. T. Price designed the gear which was (usually) driven by eccentrics between the frames, with the motion transferred to the outside cylinders through a substantial bearing, with Lap and Lead superimposed on the motion using a rod from the crosshead. The patent was held jointly by Price and Bagnall to avoid the problems caused if they parted company. The early gear had been quite satisfactory but the newer one was more sophisticated and was used on special Bagnall designs until 1953 although superseded for general use on the narrow gauge types by Walschaerts in 1915.

MARY was fitted with a proper Bagnall cab in the early days of the Second World War, presumably whilst at Stafford for boiler repairs in August 1942, returning to Cliffe Hill in September. She continued to do excellent work for the Company until that fateful day when locomotive haulage was dispensed with, and along with the rest of the stock was sold for scrap to Frank Berry in 1957.

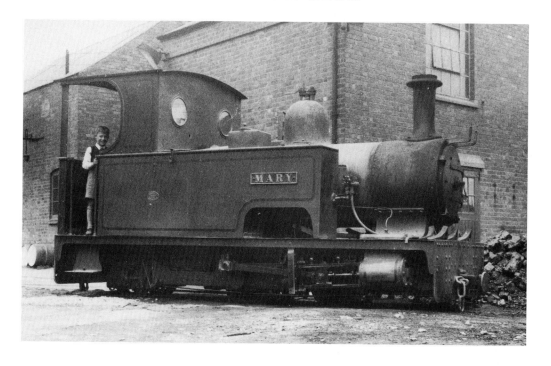

Above: Seen on 5 August 1946, by which time MARY had acquired a "proper" cab whilst at Bagnall's for repair.
Late L. W. Perkins – Collection: Maurice Billington.

Below: With a year to go before the railway closed, MARY is seen is seen in rather poor condition on 27 April 1947.
Late Bernard Roberts – Collection: Jim Peden.

Baguley's first petrol locomotive (No. 534), named GELAKEY No. 1 on test at Cliffe Hill in 1914. Collection: Rodney Weaver.

GELAKEY No. 1

Although not owned by The Cliffe Hill Granite Co., this interesting locomotive was tested at the works in 1914 by the firm of Baguley Cars Ltd. of Burton-on-Trent, prior to being exported.

Ernest E. Baguley had been Chief Draughtsman for Bagnall's for many years from 1890, but had left in 1901 to become Manager to the Ryknield Engine Co. Ltd., in Burton-on-Trent. He had later moved to the Motor Division of the mighty Birmingham Small Arms (B.S.A.) Company, which supplied engines and transmission to the Drewry Car Co. He then returned to Burton to form his own company, based in the old Ryknield works, and took over the Drewry business, together with the designs and equipment of Messrs McEwan Pratt & Co. of Wickford, Essex, pioneers of internal combustion locomotives in this country.

Baguley Cars Ltd. began trading in 1911 building railcars etc., but it was not until they took over McEwan Pratt in 1913 that they built their first locomotives for the Jokai (Assam) Tea Company who ordered four 10hp 2 feet gauge machines. The first of these, Works No. 534 and named GELAKEY No. 1 was mechanically complete in February 1914 and was sent to Markfield for testing before the final assembly of the exterior platework. The locomotive was powered by a two cylinder Baguley engine of 4in bore x 5in stroke developing 10hp at 1,000 rpm on petrol or paraffin, but unfortunately no details survive as to how the locomotive behaved at Markfield, nor have any former employees been found who could recall it. A later locomotive of the same horse power built for the War Office was able to haul 11 tons up a 1 in 100 grade in top gear at 5 mph or 10 tons up 1 in 33 at 3 mph in low gear. After the tests GELAKEY No. 1 was returned to Burton for completion, before going to the Gelakey tea estates in Assam in north-eastern India; its further history is not known.

JACK (2)

A companion locomotive to MARY was ordered on 18 December 1914 and delivered via Bardon Hill sometime in 1915. It took over the name JACK from the first locomotive of that name, which was disposed of soon afterwards. The new locomotive was Bagnall No. 2034, having larger water capacity and corresponding lower coal capacity, and different sanding gear, but otherwise

Above: JACK (second) on 21 June 1937, still very little altered from as-built condition. Some of the differences from MARY can be ascertained from the pattern of rivets on the side tanks. Late George Alliez – Collection: Allan C. Baker.

Below: Another view of the second JACK, showing signs of a different livery to that in the previous photograph. Late P. W. Robinson – Collection: Frank Jones.

identical to MARY. It was painted dark red. (See note on liveries in the description of THE ROCKET). JACK was also fitted with a bell in 1927 and her driver, Fred Cooke, rigged up a temporary wooden and tarpaulin shelter, to augment the rather skimpy weatherboard for use in wet and winter weather, it was easily removed and must have been quite an improvement although hardly an aesthetic addition. However, in 1940 a proper cab was made at the quarry, consisting of an elliptical roof, supported by two pillars at the rear and angular side sheets, but incorporating the original weatherboard which can be seen clearly on some of the photographs, both JACK and MARY were altered by Fred Boulds with smokebox door clips to ensure a tight fit and it is said that Bagnalls were so impressed that they decided to fit them as standard. For some reason, JACK was not quite as popular as MARY, but it was nevertheless a very good locomotive and worked until replaced by lorries and scrapped in January 1957.

MABEL

No more new locomotives were bought for many years, but following the war, advantage was taken of the disposal of second-hand locomotives built for war service and the Company soon added two more to its stock.

The first to arrive was MABEL in March 1920, Works No. 2077, which was another standard 6in x 9in saddle tank, but unlike CLIFFE and EDITH was fitted with Walschaerts valve gear; the "standard" design had also evolved in other minor respects by this time. This was one of a batch numbered 2076- 2080 ordered on 10 June 1918 by E. Thornton & Co., London E.C., for War Office Office Contract. No. 2077 was sent (to a Ministry of Munitions order dated 1 October

The only known close-up photograph of MABEL, seen in the shed at the quarry.
Late P. W. Robinson − Collection: Frank Jones.

1918) to Wittering Aerodrome, Stamford, Lincolnshire. After the war, Bagnall speculatively bought back a number of locomotives built for Government service, many of which were returned to Stafford for a general "cleaning up", and regauging where necessary, before sale to other customers. No. 2077, however was resold by Bagnall direct from Stamford, being dispatched to Bardon Hill Station, for Cliffe Hill Sidings, on 8 March 1920. Brass nameplates were sent on 15 March.

Apart from a tendency to lock buffers it was popular with the engine men, and many spares were supplied, the last recorded ones being in 1932. By 1942 it was in need of heavy repairs, requiring a new tank, a manhole for washing out purposes instead of merely a plug, and other items. The locomotive was returned to Bagnalls for this work to be done in December 1942, but whilst away it seems the decision to abandon the quarry lines was made and MABEL was forgotten until a phone call was received at the quarry from Bagnalls. They said that they had done the repairs as requested originally and what were the Cliffe Hill Company's further requirements? At the time the Manager, Peter Preston, was not on the premises and the only man who could tell Bagnall's anything at all was Fred Boulds, the foreman fitter, who told them that as far as he knew the locomotive would not be required any more as it had been decided to dispense with the steam engines, but that he would of course ask Mr Preston to confirm or deny this. This was done and the Stafford firm were told that all they could do was to send the locomotive back to the quarry in bits and pieces on the back of a lorry, a sad end for the locomotive for which a bill of £90 was outstanding for the repairs and alterations. As Preston later admitted to Boulds, "I had completely forgotten about it!"

The remains of MABEL were scrapped at Cliffe Hill in 1948

PETER

The next to arrive was PETER in August 1922. This locomotive had an interesting early history, which has only come to light since the First Edition of this book was written. PETER, Works No. 2067, was a standard 7in x 12in 0-4-0ST, like ISABEL but a later version, and like MABEL was fitted with Walschaerts valve gear.

Like many of the other Bagnall locomotives at Cliffe Hill, 2067 started life as part of a Stock Order, along with six others. In this case, the order was for 3ft 0in gauge machines; they were allocated Works Numbers 2067 and 2081-6. On 13 November 1918 (2 days after the Armistice was signed ending the First World War) the Ministry of Munitions ordered a further seven 3ft 0in gauge "standard" narrow gauge locomotives for forestry work, having already obtained three in 1917. Works No. 2067 was delivered on 21 December 1918 to OC 111 Company, Canadian Forestry Corps, Longtown, Cumberland. The other six in the second batch were delivered to various other Canadian Forestry Corps locations around Britain. No. 2067 is next heard of at Jane Pit Store Yard, Walker-on-Tyne where it was unsuccessfully offered for auction on 21 December 1920; at a second auction 13 August 1921, it seems to have been bought by dealer A Hammond of Boxted, Slough, but apparently not moved. Hammond sold it in January 1922 to Bagnall who must have had Cliffe Hill in mind as the eventual customer, for regauging to 2ft 0in. (They could have had a standard 6in saddle tank already to the right gauge, but wanted a 7in locomotive, and only 3ft 0in gauge machines were available). New frames, wheels, and cylinders were needed, but the cost was still less than a new locomotive. It was dispatched from Stafford to Cliffe Hill on 18 August 1922.

The parts removed from No. 2067 were put into stock, and reused for the next order for a 3ft

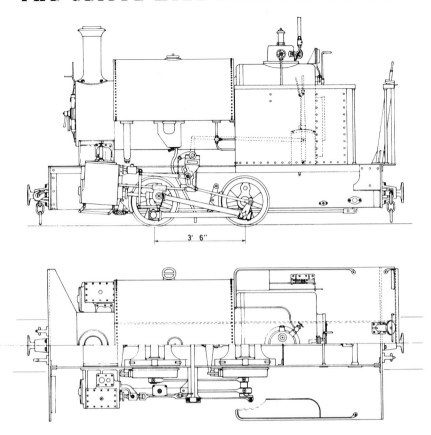

3' 6"

W. G. Bagnall Ltd. 0-4-0ST 'PETER'
Works No. 2067 - 1917

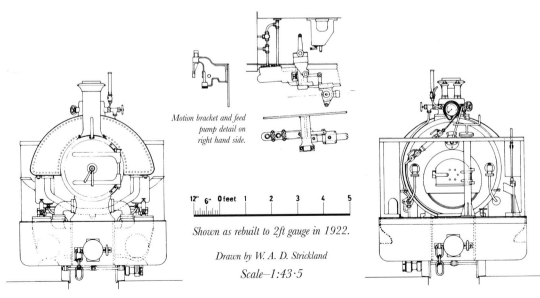

*Motion bracket and feed
pump detail on
right hand side.*

12" 6" 0 feet 1 2 3 4 5

Shown as rebuilt to 2ft gauge in 1922.

Drawn by W. A. D. Strickland

Scale—1:43·5

Above: A rear view of PETER in the quarry being driven by Mr J. Moyse (left). The remains of the lining out can be seen on the cab side sheet. Note that the square shaped object apparently on the saddle tank is in fact a chimney in the background!
Late George Alliez – Collection: Allan C. Baker.

Below: The other side of PETER at Beveridge Lane. Note the crosshead driven feed water pump, as fitted to all the Bagnall locos at Cliffe Hill. Late P. W. Robinson – Collection: Frank Jones.

Above: PETER on the spoil bank on 5 October 1950. Note that the nameplates had been moved from the tank (the only Bagnall "standard" saddle tank at Cliffe Hill to have them in that position) to the cab sides; also the deep gouge in the works plate, no doubt caused by some relatively minor accident. Three and a half years later he was presented to the Narrow Gauge Railway Society for preservation, although by then, the nameplates had disappeared.

Below: DOT, the 3ft 0in gauge locomotive (Bagnall No. 2214) built in 1923 using the parts left over when PETER was converted to 2ft 0in gauge. Photographed at Abell's Hartshill Quarry in 1950.
Both: Late Ken Cooper – Courtesy Industrial Railway Society.

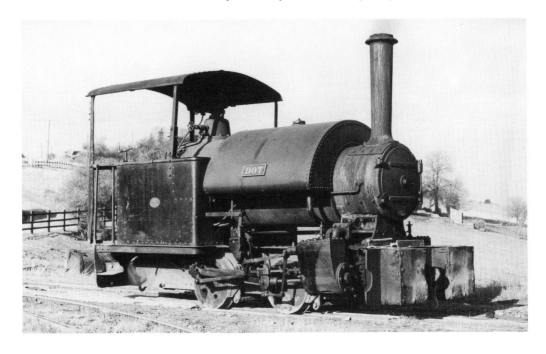

0in gauge standard 7in saddle tank. This was Works No. 2214 delivered in May 1923 to the Hartshill Granite Quarries, between Nuneaton and Atherstone, of Charles Abell Ltd. and bearing the name DOT. One month later DOT was joined by Works No. 2085 (from the same batch as PETER) which was given the name KITTY. The two locomotives lasted at Hartshill until scrapped in 1958 and 1960 respectively.

PETER's driver, Bill Read, told Maurice Billington that it was a most unpopular machine on account of its long overhang at the rear which made it very prone to "buffer locking" when the brake was applied; consequently it was little used at the quarry but used mainly at the sidings, shunting around the tarmac plant. There was no shed there until just prior to the Second World War so PETER had to travel to and from the sidings via the "main line" which must have been a bumpy ride. The locomotive worked until the end however, and although not the neatest of the Company's engines, it was to have quite a future.

The full story of PETER's preservation is told in Chapter 11, and suffice to add here that the locomotive returned briefly to Cliffe Hill from 1963 to 1965 in an abortive attempt to preserve and restore it on site.

SAMSON (later TUG)

The aforementioned stock of locomotives was quite sufficient for a few years, coping well with the increasing output, but in 1927 a new type of locomotive arrived at Cliffe Hill.

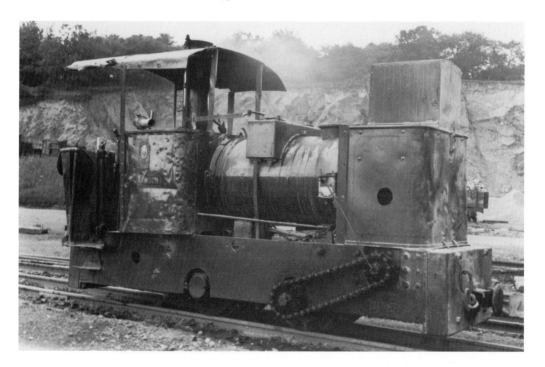

SAMSON, the Sentinel geared locomotive, seen in the quarry on 21 June 1937. Note that the boiler is mounted vertically in the cab beneath the chimney; what appear to be the "boiler" is in fact a water tank. The cylinders are also mounted vertically in the "box" at the front, with chain drive to the wheels.
Late George Alliez – Collection: Allan C. Baker.

Named SAMSON, it was ordered on 28 September 1926 for use on the main line and was one of the unusual geared locomotives based on the Sentinel road steam waggon. It was assembled by Sentinel Industrial Locomotives (England) Ltd., of Chester on behalf of, and using parts supplied by, the parent company Sentinel Waggon Works (1920) Ltd. of Shrewsbury. It was of type SIL/BE, later referred to as the "convertable" type, because the gauge could easily altered when, for example, a Contractor moved between sites. SAMSON was fitted with a superheated vertical boiler, $6^3/4$ in x 9in cylinders, chain drive, and had wheels of 1ft 8in diameter.

There is some doubt as to the correct identity of this locomotive; it carried the number 6770 at Cliffe Hill, but Sentinel's records show that No. 6751 was allocated to Cliffe Hill with the later note "This loco bears the incorrect No. plates for 6770". Both locos were being built at the same time in Chester, so it is possible that No. 6770 was completed first and diverted to Cliffe Hill to meet an urgent need.

However, according to the quarry Repair Book, it was No. 6751 which arrived at the quarry in January 1927, thus indicating another explanation.. The story told to Maurice Billington was that on the day of its trial, whilst being driven by the Sentinel test driver, the brakes failed to grip and the locomotive careered downhill and became derailed in the process, fortunately no-one was hurt, but some damage was sustained. The engine was returned to the makers for "extensive repairs" in July 1927. In the Repair Book at the quarry are two other interesting references to the locomotive, that of 8 October stating that the Bunker was straightened and that on the 13 October new brake gear and blocks were fitted after the smash. It is therefore possible that 6751 was sent to Cliffe Hill initially, but replaced by 6770 after the crash.

According to Sentinel's records, No. 6770 was allocated to the order dated 11 October 1926 from the Wigglesworth Colliery Co. Ltd. for use at their Holly Moor Colliery at Cockfield in County Durham. By June 1929 it was with the Northumberland Whinstone Co. Ltd. (some versions of the Sentinel works list indicate that it came here direct) first at Longhoughton Quarry then at Barrasford Quarry, where it was scrapped in 1957. Whilst at Barrasford, it was noted bearing plate No. 6751, confirming that the locomotives, or at least the allocated works numbers, were swapped at some stage.

Reverting to Cliffe Hill, suffice it to say that after the accident the locomotive made very occasional sorties along the railway, being confined mainly to shunting at the quarry where the ability to raise steam quickly and the increased power were much appreciated. In later years it worked almost exclusively as sidings shunter at Beveridge Lane, replacing PETER on this work.

For some reason Peter L. Preston decided to re-name the locomotive TUG in later years, although this was merely chalked on and the original nameplates removed, but as SAMSON or TUG it certainly lived up to that name, although rather slow, and was scrapped with the rest of the stud in 1957.

SOUTHSEA

In 1934 came the revolution when the workings in the "Sinking Hole" were taken over from the steam lorries by standard gauge locomotives, both came from C. J. Wills of Hayes, Middlesex, and had been used in the construction of several housing contracts in the home counties.

The first to arrive was SOUTHSEA, built by the Hunslet Engine Co., No. 215 of 1879 with 10in x 15in cylinders and 2ft 9in wheels, delivered new on 1 December 1879 to Director of Works, Portsmouth. By 1896 it was with Wills, who at the time was in partnership with Price, on their Barry Docks Contract. At Cliffe Hill it was regarded as a good locomotive, despite its age,

SOUTHSEA on 21 June 1937. This locomotive had quite a history before it arrived at Cliffe, and went on to do useful work after it left. Late George Alliez – Collection: Allan C. Baker.

and worked at there until the standard gauge rail system was abandoned, whence it passed to George Cohen, Sons & Co. Ltd. at first to their Kingsbury, Warwickshire, depot. After four years of contract work in various places it was sold to J. Varley & Sons of St. Helens, Lancashire, and was employed as yard shunter in their Waterloo Foundry. In 1952 the engine was extensively rebuilt so that in appearance at least it was very different to the one which had done such sterling work at the quarry, and finally in 1960 was scrapped by Messrs Todd Bros., a firm of scrap merchants in the town.

LORD MAYOR

Later in the same year (1934) LORD MAYOR arrived, this time the locomotive was of Hudswell Clark design, their No. 402 of 1893. It had 10in x 16in cylinders, 2ft 8in wheels and if anything was even better than the Hunslet locomotive.

LORD MAYOR had already quite a history when it came to Cliffe, first delivered to Edmund Nuttall, Ship Canal Docks, Salford (Manchester Ship Canal) on 3 July 1893 to an order of 24 June of that year, and after working there for some time was acquired by C. J. Wills and used by him on the building of the Castle Cary cut off for the G.W.R. in 1904, and it is likely that the engine worked also on the contract building the Birmingham & North Warwickshire line from Tyseley to Bearley which was finally opened in December 1907. C. J. Wills also had a hand in the construction of the great Immingham Docks for the Great Central Railway from 1906-12 and LORD MAYOR almost certainly worked on that contract. During the Great War years 1915-16, the locomotive was used by him (in the company now of two partners, Messrs Price and Reeve) on the construction on the little Spurn Head Railway, just across the Humber from Immingham but unfortunately there is a gap in the story until 1920 when the locomotive, along with three others which had worked at Spurn, was put to work on a large housing contract for the London County Council and from that year until 1934 Wills (it seems that he was again on his own) worked on a large number of similar jobs for the same authority, building estates at Becontree, Dagenham and St. Helier (Morden) whence it was sold to the quarry and worked well until 1945. Then under George Cohen's ownership, it was used on a number of contracts, one of which was the dismantling of the Liverpool Overhead Railway in 1958. Maurice Billington saw the locomotive in the shed at Stanningley in 1966, where it had lain out of use for some time, but happily in June 1968 it was presented by Cohen's to Ben Wade of Barnes, London, who had the locomotive moved to Haworth on the Keighley & Worth Valley Railway for restoration. Ben Wade and a few friends did a great deal of hard work and by March 1970 it was possible to steam again, as a superb example of a Victorian contractors engine in its green livery and much polished brasswork. It even made a brief appearance in the delightful film "The Railway Children" and as a result of that is likely to be the best known locomotive that ever worked at Cliffe Hill, although the majority would not know of this fact. At the time of writing (February 1997) LORD MAYOR is on static display at Oxenhope Station (K&WVLR), although it is normally kept in the Vintage Carriage Trust's Museum at Ingrow.

LORD MAYOR also had the distinction of being the subject for a superb 5in gauge model built by two brothers, W. A. and P. J. Dupen of Dagenham, Essex, who had remembered the

The other standard gauge locomotive, LORD MAYOR, also being loaded by an excavator in the "Sinking Hole".
Collection: Maurice Billington.

EDITH, the second locomotive to carry the name, and the second one of its type at Cliffe Hill. Seen in the shed on 27 April 1947. Late Bernard Roberts – Collection: Jim Peden.

locomotive well whilst working on the Wills contract there, the model was commenced in 1936 but was not completed until some time after the war, W. A. Dupen unfortunately being killed in an air raid on London in 1944. The model was deservedly the Championship Cup winner at the Model Engineering exhibition in 1950 and in the following year was also exhibited at the Festival of Britain on the South Bank, London, where it was admired by Maurice Billington, painted in deep "Midland" red with much polished brasswork.

EDITH (2)

Reverting to the Narrow Gauge a further locomotive came to Cliffe Hill in 1935, and was another Sentinel geared locomotive, but this time second-hand. This was No. 6902 of 1927, another "convertable" locomotive, identical to SAMSON, but built by the Sentinel Waggon Works at Shrewsbury. It came from the Durham County Water Board, who had used it on the construction of Burnhope Reservoir, one of the last contracts to use a large fleet of narrow gauge steam locomotives. The locomotive was ordered from Sentinel by the Leeds dealer, J. C. Oliver, but it is likely that they were only acting as agents for the Water Board.

At Cliffe Hill the locomotive originally had no name but was soon fitted with the plate off the redundant EDITH. This was another powerful locomotive but rather prone to derailment until Fred Boulds effected some alterations to the under frame plate, which had been fitted whilst up in Durham in order to make the frame more rigid. In fact, however satisfactory it might have been on the reservoir job, it was not nearly flexible enough for the quarry line. The alterations, which

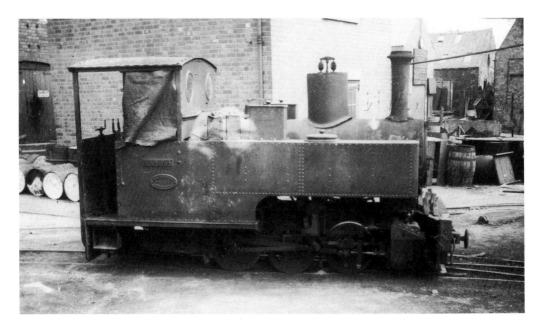

KASHMIR, the only six coupled locomotive at Cliffe Hill. Note the very long overhang at the rear. Sister locomotive SGT MURPHEY has had a pony truck added in preservation for stability. Late Bernard Roberts – Collection: Jim Peden.

consisted of cutting away part of the plate made the locomotive quite suitable and it worked until the end, being scrapped in 1957 with all the remaining stock.

KASHMIR

The last steam engine to be delivered to the quarry did not arrive until 1941, this was one of the standard Kerr Stuart 0-6-0T's known as the "Haig" class, Works No. 3118. The "Haig" class originated in the First World War with an order from the French Government for an 0-6-0T closely based on those built by Decauville with $8^{1}/_{2}$in x 11in cylinders. Several batches of these "Decauville" class (sometimes known as the "Joffre" class) were built, and Kerr Stuart started another batch, anticipating a further order which did not materialise. To make use of these parts, they conceived the "Haig" class, very similar but of a more angular appearance than the rounded French design.

A batch of six Haig class locomotives was ordered for stock on 14 February 1918 (Bagnall were not the only firm to indulge in this practice!), and allocated Works Nos. 3115-3120. Four of them were for 3ft 0in gauge, but 3117 and 3118 were 2ft 0in, the only Haigs of this gauge for use in this country. Both were purchased by the Ministry of Munitions in November 1918, and No. 3118 was sent by rail to Officer Commanding, 35th Wing, Royal Airforce, Stamford, Lincolnshire. Here it must have worked alongside Bagnall No. 2077, which later became MABEL at Cliffe Hill.

After aerodrome construction service Kerr Stuart No. 3118 was transferred to the Home Grown Timber Committee and worked extracting timber on a revived section of the old Kerry Tramway near Newtown in Montgomeryshire arriving on 11 March 1920. The tramway closed again in 1922 or 1923, and in December 1925 No. 3118 was bought by Richard Costain Ltd. for building a housing estate near Croydon, Surrey. In 1928 3118 was owned by dealers William

Jones Ltd. of Greenwich, who resold it to Surrey County Council in September 1931. It was numbered GP76, and used on the construction of the Hogs Back section of the Guildford bypass, upon completion of which it was auctioned with other equipment on 21/22 November 1934. The purchaser was Charlton Sand & Ballast Co. Ltd. whose pits were at Littleton near Shepperton in Middlesex, but it saw little use there, being advertised for sale in "Machinery Market" several times between 1936 and 1939.

The Cliffe Hill Co. bought No. 3118 in 1941 and named it KASHMIR as has already been related. It proved to be a good steamer and powerful, but was even worse than PETER at "riding the trucks" when the brakes were applied, and had to be eased off very gently in reverse. A trial was made with fitting "Follsain" brake blocks, consisting of a very hard compound made by the Follsain Co. at their works at Cosby, Leicestershire. These were very long lasting but the "bite" was not there, even after they had been roughened, and so the conventional blocks had to be reverted to. In spite of its faults the locomotive worked until the end and was scrapped by F. Berry in 1957.

Incidentally, sister locomotive 3117, became SGT. MURPHEY at Penrhyn Slate Quarry, and is now well known since being restored privately for use on the Ffestiniog Railway, although it was moved in 1996 to the Vale of Teifi Railway near Cardigan in South Wales..

Orenstein & Koppel Diesel

The only other locomotive to work at Cliffe Hill was a small diesel locomotive of the "Montania" type, purchased from the dealer Thomas W. Ward Ltd., Albion Works, Sheffield. The Montania locomotives were built by Orenstein & Koppel of Berlin, and imported into this country by William Jones Ltd. of London. The Cliffe Hill locomotive's identity is not known, but it was probably one of a batch of six of these locomotives that Ward's bought on 15 January 1938 from John Gill Contractors Ltd. from a site at Goole.

Of these six locomotives, five (Works Nos. 5121 and 5126 of 1935, and 5479, 6133 and 6134 of 1936) were of the RL1b type, and the sixth (Works No. 4104 of 1931) was of the earlier RL1a class. Ward's initially hired out all six locomotives to various customers, but sales to new owners

'Montania' diesel locomotive, type RL1b as illustrated in a William Jones catalogue sheet. Collection: D. Smith.

were only recorded for Nos. 5479 and 6133, so that any of the other four are candidates for the Cliffe Hill machine.

Little is known of the exploits of this locomotive, and in fact only one of the former employees at the quarry could remember it and he was not at all enthusiastic about the machine. It spent most of its time at the Tarmac plant at the quarry and was used as little as possible, having an unenviable record for both starting and derailment. There was no protection for the driver and was regarded as a bad investment. It was noted in a very dark shed by Maurice Billington in June 1950 (but unfortunately not recorded or photographed) and must have been sold soon after to a scrap dealer named Burgess whose whereabouts has not been discovered, and so the fate of the locomotive is not known.

Rolling Stock

There were three basic types of wagon in use at Cliffe Hill. All were side tipping types (i.e. the body could tip to discharge the load, relative to the underframe); early ones had rectangular bodies, some all metal, and some with wooden bodies lined with metal. Later ones had "V" shaped bodies, but with inside bearing wheelsets, rather than the conventional outside frames.

Study of records has not revealed all the details of these wagons, but many were supplied by W. G. Bagnall Ltd., who specialised in supplying complete railways, and not just locomotives (they supplied rail and metal sleepers to Cliffe Hill as well). Included in the order with CLIFFE and ISABEL were some 45 cubic feet side tipping wagons, and 40 cu ft wood side tip wagons lined in steel, numbers not specified. In 1923, an unspecified number of Skips, with dimensions 5ft 6in x 4ft-0in, were supplied by Bagnall, together with some 45 cu ft drop side tip wagons with 17in wheels. In 1924 3 more skips were supplied, together with 30 drop side tip wagons with 17in diameter wheels, 2ft-3 in wheelbase, and 45 cu ft capacity were supplied; another 50 of the same design followed in 1926.

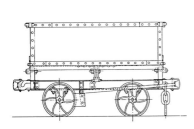
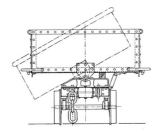

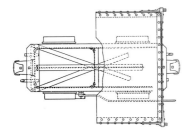

SIDE TIPPING WAGON

Scale – 1:43·5

Drawn by Alan Kidner, 1982.
Based on an original 1892 'Works Drawing'.

Other wagons came from J & F Howard of Bedford, but in later years the majority of them came from Hadfields Ltd., of Sheffield (who had quoted as early as 1899), Bradley Bros. of Dudley, and W. G. Allen & Sons of Tipton.

There was also a rail mounted crane, suitable for breakdown use, as recalled in one of the anecdotes described in the next Chapter. However no further details have come to light.

CLIFFE HILL GRANITE CO. – LOCOMOTIVES

NARROW (2ft 0in) GAUGE

Name	Wheel Arrangement	Maker	Works No.	Date	Origin	Disposal
CLIFFE	0-4-0ST	WB	1487	1896	New	(1)
ISABEL	0-4-0ST	WB	1491	1897	New	(2)
THE ROCKET	0-4-0ST	WB	1531	1898	New	Scr.1957
EDITH (1)	0-4-0ST	WB	1589	1900	New	Scr.c.1935
JACK (1)	0-4-0ST	WB	1650	1901	New	(3)
MARY	0-4-2T	WB	1943	1911	New	Scr.1957
GELAKEY No.1	0-4-0PM	Bg	534	1914	(a)	(4)
JACK (2)	0-4-2T	WB	2034	1915	New	Scr.1957
MABEL	0-4-0ST	WB	2077	1918	(b)	Scr.c.1948
PETER	0-4-0ST	WB	2067	1918	(c)	(5)
SAMSON (later TUG)	4wGVBT	S	6770	1926	New	Scr.1957
–	4wGVBT	S	6751	1926	(see text)	(see text)
EDITH (2)	4wGVBT	S	6902	1927	(d)	Scr.1957
KASHMIR	0-6-0T	KS	3118	1918	(e)	Scr.1957
–	4wDM	OK	*	*	(f)	(6)

– One of Works Nos. 4104/1931, 5121/1935, 5126/1935, or 6134/1936.

STANDARD GAUGE

Name	Wheel Arrangement	Maker	Works No.	Date	Origin	Disposal
SOUTHSEA	0-4-0ST	HE	215	1879	(g)	(7)
LORD MAYOR	0-4-0ST	HC	402	1893	(h)	(8)

NOTES

Locomotive Makers

Bg   Baguley Cars Ltd., Burton-on-Trent.
HC   Hudswell Clarke & Co., The Railway Foundry, Leeds.
HE   Hunslet Engine Co. Ltd, Jack Lane, Leeds.
KS   Kerr Stuart & Co. Ltd., California Works, Stoke-on-Trent.
OK   Orenstein & Koppel AG, Berlin. Sold in Britain by William Jones Ltd., London.
S   Sentinel Waggon Works Ltd., Battlefield, Shrewsbury.
WB   W. G. Bagnall Ltd., Castle Engine Works, Stafford.

Origin of Locomotives

New   Supplied direct from the maker concerned, usually in the year of manufacture.
(a)   From Makers, on test only, February 1914.
(b)   From Ministry of Munitions, Stamford Aerodrome, Lincs., 3/1920, per W. G. Bagnall.
(c)   From W. G. Bagnall, 8/1922. Originally built for Ministry of Munitions. (see Chapter 9).
(d)   From Durham County Water Board, 1935
(e)   From Charlton Sand & Ballast Co., Shepperton, Middlesex, 1941. Originally with Ministry of Munitions, Stamford Aerodrome.

(f)   From Thomas W. Ward, Sheffield, c.1940.
(g)   From C. J. Wills, Hayes, Middlesex, 1934. Originally with Director of Works, Portsmouth.
(h)   From C. J. Wills, Hayes, Middlesex, 1934. Originally with Edmund Nuttall, Salford.

Disposal of Locomotives
Scr.   Scrapped on site on date shown.
(1)   To Ellis & Everard, Bardon Hill Quarry, Leicestershire, 1946. (Scrapped c.1953).
(2)   To W. G. Bagnall, Stafford for preservation, 3/1953. (For further information see Chapter 12).
(3)   To Graham's Moor Quarry Co., Criggion, Montgomeryshire, 6/1916.
(4)   To N.G.R.S. c/o W. G. Bagnall, Stafford for preservation, 1954. (Returned to Cliffe Hill 1963-1965, for further information see Chapter 11).
(5)   Returned to makers, thence to Jokai (Assam) Tea Co., India. Final disposal unknown.
(6)   Disposal unknown. Presumed scrapped on site 1957.
(7)   To George Cohen, Sons & Co., Kingsbury, Warwickshire, 1948. Finally scrapped 1960.
(8)   To George Cohen, Sons & Co., unknown location, 1948. Now preserved on the Keighley & Worth Valley Railway, Yorkshire.

JACK (second) awaiting his fate on the spoil bank, 8 October 1950. By this time the original weatherboard (which was retained) had a roof and sides added to form a rudimentary cab for the crew.
Late Ken Cooper – Courtesy Industrial Railway Society.

TABLE OF LOCOMOTIVE DIMENSIONS

Name	Maker and No.	Type	Cylinder Size and Position (in.)	Valve Gear Type	Driving Wheel Dia. (ft-in)	Other Wheel Dia. (ft-in)	Coupled W.base (ft-in)	Total W.base (ft-in)
CLIFFE	WB1487	0-4-0ST	6 x 9 OC	(1)	1-6	–	3-0	3-0
ISABEL	WB1491	0-4-0ST	7 x12 OC	(1)	1-9^1/$_2$	–	3-6	3-6
THE ROCKET	WB1531	0-4-0ST	7 x12 OC	(1)	1-9^1/$_2$	–	3-6	3-6
EDITH (1)	WB1589	0-4-0ST	6 x 9 OC	(1)	1-7	–	3-0	3-0
JACK (1)	WB1650	0-4-0ST	7 x12 OC	(1)	1-9^1/$_2$	–	3-6	3-6
MARY	WB1943	0-4-2T	8 x12 OC	(2)	2-0^1/$_2$	1-7	3-7	9-1
JACK (2)	WB2034	0-4-2T	8 x12 OC	(2)	2-0^1/$_2$	1-7	3-7	9-1
MABEL	WB2077	0-4-0ST	6 x 9 OC	(3)	1-7	–	3-6	3-6
PETER	WB20677	0-4-0ST	7 x 12 OC	(3)	1-9^1/$_2$	–	3-6	3-6
SAMSON	S6770	4wGVBT	6^3/$_4$ x 9 V	?	1-8	–	?	?
EDITH (2)	S6902	4wGVBT	6^3/$_4$ x 9 V	?	1-8	–	?	?
KASHMIR	KS3118	0-6-0T	8^1/$_2$ x11 OC	(3)	1-11^5/$_8$	–	2-3^9/$_{16}$	4-7^1/$_4$
–	OK?	4wDM	4^3/$_8$ x 6^3/$_4$ D	–	1-6	–	2-6^3/$_4$	2-6^3/$_4$
SOUTHSEA	HE215	0-4-0ST	10 x15 OC	(4)	2-9	–	4-9	4-9
LORD MAYOR	HC402	0-4-0ST	10 x16 OC	(4)	2-9	–	5-6	5-6

TABLE OF LOCOMOTIVE DIMENSIONS - cont'd

Water Capacity (gal.)	Fuel Capacity (cu.ft.)	Weight Working Order (tons)	Working Pressure (p.s.i.)	Firebox Type	Heating Surface Tubes (sq.ft.)	Heating Surface Firebox (sq.ft.)	Heating Surface TOTAL (sq.ft.)	Grate Area (sq.ft.)
104	5	5.5	140	(B)	80	9.77	89.77	3.28
200	5	6.25	140	(B)*	118	12.5	130.5	4
200	5.3	6.25	150	(C)	117	21	138	3.95
100	5	5.5	140	(B)	80	9.77	89.77	3.28
200	5.3	6.25	150	(C)	117	21	138	3.95
200	21	12.25	160	(C)	165	32	197	6.66
260	10.5	12.25	160	(C)	165	32	197	6.66
100	6	5.5	150	(B)	80	9	89	3.25
150	7	7.5	150	(B)	115	13	128	4.2
?	?	?	?	?	?	?	?	?
?	?	?	?	?	?	?	?	?
264	22	10.5	160	(C)	168.5	23.25	191.75	4
–	–	3	–	–	–	–	–	–
300	13	13·5	120	(C)	257	32	289	5·5
360	?	15.75	130	(C)	243.13	30.47	273.6	4.5

NOTES

A dash (–) indicates that this column does not apply to the locomotive concerned. A question mark (?) indicates that the information is not known.

For manufacturer abbreviations, see "Locomotives" table.

Cylinders – Dimensions shown are Diameter x Stroke; OC Outside cylinders; V vertical cylinders; D single cylinder diesel.

Valve Gear Types – (1) Baguley "Patent"; (2) Bagnall-Price; (3) Walschaerts; (4) Stephenson.

Firebox Types – (B) "Bull-Head" (circular); (C) Conventional locomotive type; * as built, see text.

CHAPTER TEN
ACCIDENTS AND ANECDOTES

QUARRYING IS A DANGEROUS OCCUPATION and in spite of a good record the Cliffe Hill Company did not escape accidents altogether, fortunately there were no fatalities on the tramway but there were several near misses.

On one occasion Jabez Bilson, who was locomotive foreman for many years, told the regular driver, Joe Orton, that he would take over on MARY for the run down to the sidings, and it seems that he was so eager to make a good speed that he could not stop at the head of the gradient to put the skids under the wheels. The train careered down the line at full speed, fortunately it was not derailed but when the news reached Mr Preston he had to severely reprimand Mr Bilson.

MARY was involved in another accident at the Beveridge Lane crossing, and this time the train was well and truly derailed. It seems that the track at that time was not chaired and in taking the sharp curve when immediately across the road the rails must have spread. The locomotive was derailed followed by several wagons which were fortunately empty at the time, however the breakdown crane with THE ROCKET in charge had to be sent for. To make matters worse the accident happened at night and the job of re-railing had to be carried out by the light of acetylene lamps.

Beveridge Lane was the only really major road crossed by the railway, and it is indeed fortunate that no serious accident occurred there as there were no resident flagmen. The job of seeing the train across the road had to be performed by the engine men and in foggy weather, with the road further obscured by smoke, it could have been dangerous, in spite of whistles or bells being used.

In the very early days lights were not used except on the locomotives, and these which were of the "Colza" type did not provide much illumination, although they could be seen by other people. In later years Acetylene lamps were provided and were a great improvement, projecting quite a beam, but the wagons were without lights until the Police made a request that they be provided to warn those in charge of road vehicles that a train was crossing the road ahead. Such an accident did in fact happen some years later at the crossing of the minor road at Battleflat just beyond the loop, when a motor cyclist did run into a wagon, but this must have been a case of negligence as it happened in broad daylight. He was very lucky, sustaining only a cut forehead for his pains.

The Company had its share of characters too, in the very early days when schooling was by no means universal, many of the men could not read or write anything beyond their names, sometimes not even that, and as it was the practice for all employees to sign a book at the "signing on clock". They had to use various signs to denote their presence, such as a cross, a circle, or triangle. In addition those quarrymen who were paid by the load had also to sign a chit to denote who was responsible and as at one time there were seven men with the same surname and five each having two other names, the surname would not be much use to the clerk who had to calculate the pay, so by common consent it was decided to use the men's nicknames instead and such choice names as "Chad", "Squib", "Dump", "Toddler", and "Flannel" began to appear in the Company's books.

Another likeable fellow was one "Porgy" Orgill, who was employed as a shunter on the tramway, and he had quite a gift for playing the ukelele. During the summer it was no uncommon thing for the water supply to fail at the quarry and trains consisting of water tanks on trucks had to run down to the well to be filled and transported back to the quarry in order to replenish the tanks there. These trains were normally run throughout the night but inevitably there were times when they just had to be run whilst loaded trains were still being worked to the sidings and of course these trains had the right of way so the water train would have to go into the loop at Battleflat and there wait until the loaded train had passed. On these occasions "Porgy" would fetch out his ukelele and strum away happily.

Up to the time of the Second World War it was common for the children of the employees during their break from school to take their father's dinner in a basin to the cabin where they ate, and one of the men, "Brunner" Wood, who was a staunch union man, told the children that it was worth more than the customary 3d per week for all the walking involved and that they ought to demand 6d from their fathers. This was done but their fathers did not agree to this increase so the youngsters went on strike for a week until their claims were agreed to – it seems to have been successful too, but it must have caused some feeling between the fathers and their children and even more so towards "Brunner" Wood.

One man was quite an exhibitionist and if his meal did not suit him he would throw it over the rafters inside the cabin, the comments of his workmates at this behaviour, or who had to clean up the mess afterwards, is best left to the imagination.

The characters were not all of the human variety either, for there was the story of the pony who went on strike for a day. It seems that in the early days of the Company a pony was bought to assist in getting loaded tubs away from the mills. It very soon accustomed itself to the work which was to pull the loaded wagons to the marshalling area in readiness for locomotives to draw away to the sidings. After being harnessed in his stable, he would make his own way to the mills and turn round with his back to the first wagon. After hooking on he would start on his short journey without any word from the loader, picking his way over the various points and carefully stepping off the track after giving the final pull. On hearing the boy loader remove the hook from the wagon, he would return to the mills for his next load. A word from the ostler when he opened the field gate at the beginning of the day was quite sufficient to bring him up to work, except on one occasion when the ostler did not turn up for the morning shift. The loader from the mill went to call him but he just sat down on his haunches refusing to move, in spite of all efforts and bribes, until the right man called him. He then came in his usual quiet manner and after harnessing, went to his work in the normal way. A real sit-down strike, and incidentally, the only strike in the history of the Company.

CHAPTER ELEVEN
PRESERVATION OF PETER

After its travels around the country, PETER returned to Cliffe Hill in 1963,
and is seen across the road from the quarry office.
Collection: Maurice Billington.

IN CHAPTER NINE, we saw how PETER survived in use to the end of railway operations at Cliffe Hill. It subsequently became one of the earliest private locomotive preservation projects, and almost certainly the most widely travelled.

Eric G. Cope, who founded the Narrow Gauge Railway Society in Leeds in 1951, was most anxious that they should own a small locomotive, and after hearing of the Cliffe Hill engines being stored he visited the quarry and expressed interest in the locomotive ISABEL. It transpired that its original manufacturer, W. G. Bagnall were themselves interested in the older engine, so Mr Cope, who had by this time interested a few of his fellow Society members in the idea of preservation, approached the Cliffe Hill Company and PETER was duly presented to Mr Cope on behalf of the N.G.R.S. in March 1954. It had also been arranged that Bagnall would store the locomotive for the Society and when funds became available to pay for the work of restoration they (Bagnall) would do it; unfortunately the money for preservation did not flow in to the Society coffers and Bagnall was no longer able to keep it on their premises so asked Mr Cope if he could have it removed. several homes were suggested for it, one of which was at Nailstone, Leicestershire, on the premises of Mr R. S. King, a Society member who had lived at Battleflat and knew the locomotive well. However, a home was found in one of the private firms at Yeadon Aerodrome (now Leeds Bradford Airport), and it was moved there in 1957.

In 1958 the sponsors of the Lincolnshire Coast Light Railway at Humberstone, near Cleethorpes, were anxious to obtain a steam locomotive for use on their railway and Mr Cope was equally anxious to find a more permanent home for the engine. So PETER was moved again in October 1958 to the home at Fotherby, Louth, of Bill Woolhouse of the L.C.L.R.

At this time the Lincolnshire Coast Light Railway had not been laid, nor had the plans for the layout been finalised but by spring 1960 these had been settled and the line opened in August of that year, however PETER remained in the shed at Fotherby until spring 1961 when it was again moved, this time to the North Sea Lane shed at Humberstone.

Whilst at Fotherby the locomotive had been thoroughly examined but it was found to be needing much more attention, with all its attendant cost, than had at first been thought, also by this time the Peckett locomotive JURASSIC had been bought and it was decided by the directors that unless PETER could actually become the property of the L.C.L.R. that it would not be a justifiable expense.

The N.G.R.S. however, could not sell the engine as it had been given to them by the Cliffe Hill Company and it was still hoped to have it working eventually on the Society's own line. Whilst on loan to the L.C.L.R. a cab for the locomotive had been purchased from the Penrhyn Quarries

PETER being moved by the quarry's breakdown lorry, prior to travel to Brockham Museum.
Tony Deller – Collection: David H Smith.

Ltd. of Bethesda, North Wales, from their locomotive SGT. MURPHY (which as already noted, was the sister locomotive of KASHMIR at Cliffe Hill!). Peter McHowell Preston expressed his interest in the locomotive to Maurice Billington who had told him of its whereabouts, and he (Mr Preston) contacted the Lincolnshire Coast Light Railway board with a view to arranging its return to Cliffe Hill where he hoped to have it as the main attraction of a quarry museum he was contemplating, with the full concurrence of the N.G.R.S. PETER duly travelled back to its old home, but unfortunately Mr Preston died suddenly in May 1963 and he never saw the locomotive. It was stored in the open at the quarry, just across the road from the office, but in view of the impending sale of the Cliffe Hill Company into the mighty Tarmac group nothing was done to it.

John Townsend, the energetic Museum Secretary of the N.G.R.S., contacted the Company and asked if the locomotive could be moved again, this time to the Society Museum at Brockham near Dorking in Surrey where it was hoped to provide a permanent home. The Cliffe Hill Company agreed to this and in August 1965 it was transported on the back of a low loader via the M1 motorway.

The Museum at Brockham was established as a result of the acquisition by the N.G.R.S. of the 3ft $2^1/_4$in gauge locomotive TOWNSEND HOOK from the Betchworth Quarry of the Dorking Greystone Lime Co. (The Society has been directly responsible for the preservation of five steam locomotives, PETER and TOWNSEND HOOK, discussed here, together with three locomotives which found a home at the Leeds Industrial Museum). A temporary base was made at the Bluebell Railway in Sussex, but this, the first standard gauge preserved railway, was not really very suitable for a narrow gauge locomotive, so a place was found at Brockham, only a mile from its original home at Betchworth. The site was in a disused chalk pit, and as soon as it was available, it seemed to be an ideal site for a "national" museum of narrow gauge railways. Over the years, a large collection of steam, petrol, diesel, and electric locomotives, coaches, wagons, and other relics was obtained. Buildings were restored to house some of the collection (although most of it had to remain in the open air), and a short 2ft 0in gauge (being the most common, although many other gauges were represented in the collection) demonstration railway was built. The administration of the Museum was soon separated from the N.G.R.S. and eventually a Charitable Trust (the Brockham Museum Trust) took over. At an early stage, PETER was selected for full restoration to become the first operational steam locomotive on the 2ft 0in gauge line. However, continuing the "tradition" of having work started but not finished by successive keepers, PETER was put to one side when POLAR BEAR was acquired in 1967, and very little further work was done at Brockham. The site had one major drawback as a "public" museum, and that was the access, being up a dirt track off a busy trunk road, neither aspect being suitable for visitors. The establishment of the Trust created a legal obligation to open to the public, and the conflict had to be resolved eventually.

After 20 years at Brockham, the situation was resolved by moving the entire collection to the newly established Chalk Pits Museum at Amberley, near Arundel in West Sussex.

The Chalk Pits Museum at Amberley (more recently it has been known simply as the Amberley Museum) was opened to the public in 1979, and was described as "an open air Museum where the Industrial History of the South East can be Studied and Preserved". It is perhaps best considered as a collection of collections; these including Southdown buses (the local bus company) with a replica bus garage; printing workshop; country timber yard; and various craftsmen ranging from potter to boat builder. More recently the Museum became the home of the Milne

PETER on the day it was delivered to Brockham Museum in August 1965.
It was dismantled soon afterwards, and was moved in 1982 in that state to the Chalk Pits Museum, Amberley.
Andrew Neale.

Collection, effectively the South Eastern Electricity Board (SEEBoard) "official" museum of electrical equipment and appliances.

A small collection of industrial narrow gauge railway equipment had already been gathered, mostly from local sources, when it was suggested that the Brockham Collection should come to Amberley. The move took place between 1981 and 1983; PETER itself moving early in 1982.

The first 2ft.0in. gauge steam locomotive working at Amberley was POLAR BEAR, followed shortly afterwards by BARBOULIER, the Decauville 0-4-0T privately owned by Peter Smith. A number of internal combustion engined locomotives were also restored, probably the most difficult and thorough being PELDON, the John Fowler 4w diesel which had been acquired in a derelict state with the engine seized up. The person responsible for this work was Doug Bentley, assisted by his son Dave; and this team was looking for another challenge once PELDON was complete. It was decided to make a start on PETER, on the basis that the mechanical work could be done fairly cheaply, and worry about finding the money for the boiler work at a later date – and if that was not forthcoming, at least a cosmetic restoration would result, much better than the pile of bits! Another Amberley volunteer, Bill Johnston, joined the team at this stage.

Full restoration work started on PETER during February 1989, with the complete stripping of the engine to the bare frames. Repairs to the frames included replacing corroded angles and rivets, thorough cleaning and painting. As rebuilding work continued, it was found that the right hand radius rod, expansion link and die block were missing. A new radius rod was made to the

PETER, seen from above, undergoing restoration at Amberley. The frames and cab side sheets are nearly complete, and the rebuilt boiler is awaited. David H Smith.

pattern of the left-hand rod. A used spare expansion link was obtained from Patrick Keef of Alan Keef Ltd., (who had just completed the restoration of a similar "7 inch" Bagnall saddle tank No. 2133, called WOTO, originally from the British Insulated Callenders Cables works at Erith in Kent. The spare expansion link was stamped 2053 which meant that it came from another Bagnall at B.I.C.C. Erith, named THE MIGHTY ATOM). Although the radius rod was correct, the driving eye position was wrong. This was cut off, and a new section was welded in place and reprofiled, drilled and reamed to size and hardened. A new expansion die block was made and fitted. Rebuilding of all the valve gear was then completed with new bushes and hardened pins etc., as required. New cab side sheets and rear handrails were needed (because the originals had been scrapped when it was proposed to fit SGT MURPHY's cab at Louth), and the saddle tank was beyond repair. The spare, welded, tank from the ISABEL project was purchased by the N.G.R.S. and this has been modified where necessary and fitted to PETER.

Work on the "chassis" was well under way when sponsorship for the boiler work was offered and accepted; the money was provided in memory of the husband of Mrs Cheryl Tipton (a member of Bill Johnston's family) and is commemorated by a brass plaque on the cab side. The repairs to the boiler were carried out by the Chatham Steam Restoration Co. (situated within the historic Chatham Dockyard in Kent), including a new smokebox, front tube plate, tubes and other assorted work including cutting out a section of the underside of the wrapper plate and welding a new section in. The boiler returned to Amberley on 17 March 1993. Completion was then rapid, with the locomotive being used for the first time in September 1993 on freight trains only. Power brakes, suitable for passenger work, were fitted over the following winter, and PETER was used on passenger trains for the first time on 1 and 2 May 1994.

PETER has been painted in the original Bagnall livery of dark Brunswick green lined in black and yellow.

On 22 May 1994, the Chairman of the Narrow Gauge Railway Society, Ron Redman, ceremonially unveiled a plaque indicating their ownership of the locomotive, thus effectively marking the completion of the restoration of PETER.

As part of the celebrations for the centenary of ISABEL, plans are being formed at the time of writing for PETER to visit the latter's home in May 1997 in company with a number of other Bagnall locomotives.

With restoration and painting completed, PETER is seen in steam at Amberley on 1 May 1994, the occasion being the Museum's "Railway Weekend". POLAR BEAR and BARBOULIER visible to the right.
Doug Bentley.

CHAPTER ELEVEN
PRESERVATION OF ISABEL

ISABEL on its plinth at the Bagnall works in Stafford, The background has been painted out in this "Official" view.
Collection: Maurice Billington.

I F PETER'S TRAVELS IN PRESERVATION hands have been both extensive and complicated, ISABEL's story is much simpler. It will be recalled from Chapter Eight that in March 1952, ISABEL was sold to her makers, W. G. Bagnall at Castle Engine Works, Stafford. She had been bought from the Cliffe Hill Company as an early example of one of their products and was to be put on display in their works yard. she was cosmetically restored by the apprentices of the day and other employees as an "infill" job. As this work was being undertaken, the very final steam locomotive of this design (i.e. the circular firebox saddle tank) was being erected. This was Works No. 3051 (of 1953) and the direct lineage was obvious in a design spanning nearly 60 years.

During 1953 ISABEL was placed on a plinth near the factory entrance as a memorial to the two thousand locomotives built by Bagnalls over the years and she remained there until the take over of the Company by English Electric in June 1961. Unfortunately a decision was made to cease locomotive production in Stafford which left ISABEL with a somewhat uncertain future.

A chance communication with the works by a local enthusiast regarding the old Bagnall records and other artifacts led to the offer of a complete 2ft gauge locomotive! Some quick thinking prompted an approach to the Town Council and ultimately a suitable site was agreed where ISABEL could be put on display.

Members of the Stafford Railway Circle undertook some basic cosmetic restoration prior to her being placed on a plinth once again, this time in Victoria Park adjacent to the new Stafford Railway Station. She was finally accepted on behalf of the Borough of Stafford by the then Mayor, Rees Tyler in a ceremony held in 1963.

ISABEL then settled down to a fairly quiet life in the park where she was played upon by probably every youngster in Stafford, becoming a bit of a landmark in the town. She was attended to every now and then by local enthusiasts but being out in the open, the weather inevitably took its toll.

By 1977, ISABEL was looking a little worse for wear and the Council decided to restore her, so she returned to the Castle Works, by now part of GEC, to be attended to by the apprentices there. At this time she appeared to loose one or two of her fittings, some during the restoration work whilst others had apparently disappeared during her time in the park.

ISABEL emerged newly painted and lined out to take up a new position opposite the station

By 1975, ISABEL was on this plinth in Victoria Park (opposite the Station) in Stafford.
Cosmetically it appeared in good condition, having recently been repainted. David H. Smith.

during jubilee year. It says much for the people of Stafford that she was spared the damaging vandalism that is so prevalent in our times. However nothing could protect her from the elements and by the early 1980's, her chimney had collapsed through corrosion and frost damage and her general condition had deteriorated making her a very sorry sight indeed.

Something had to be done and in 1984 ISABEL remarkably returned yet again to Castle Works to be dismantled by trainees there on a work experience scheme. This action at least got the loco under cover but the Council was very unsure as what to do with her. Two options appeared to be open, either to carry out a full restoration, or a purely cosmetic facelift; either way the Council would be left with a problem of where to put her, certainly the old plinth would not be satisfactory.

Around this time a local businessman, Martyn Smythe, approached the Council and an agreement was drawn up in 1985 whereby Mr Smythe would undertake restoration of the locomotive to full working order for eventual display and operation at the 1986 National Garden Festival at Stoke-on-Trent. The Council agreed to provide some funding and the boiler was dispatched to the works of Roger Pridham in Cornwall for repairs. Meanwhile the dismantled remains were moved to Mr Smythe's premises and work commenced on the frames and running gear.

Subsequently, the restoration was to run into problems, delays occurred and by mid 1986 the Trust Fund set up by the Council had been disbanded, restoration eventually ground to a halt with numerous difficulties arising between Mr Smythe and the Council. By October of that year, ISABEL was in three locations, the Council had the frames, wheels and cab, Mr Smythe had the new saddle tank and various valve gear parts and the boiler remained at Pridham's.

It was at this time that ISABEL's predicament came to the notice of a local enthusiast, Phil Jones, who had been following the progress of the little Bagnall with interest, and on 9 October 1986, Phil arranged a meeting in Stafford for those interested in continuing and completing the restoration of ISABEL. A new body entitled the Staffordshire Narrow Gauge Advisory Group put a fresh initiative to the Council and by the beginning of 1987 a new Company had been formed. This was The Staffordshire Narrow Gauge Railway Society Ltd., which ultimately reached a formal agreement with Stafford Borough Council in October of that year. ISABEL was saved.

It was fortuitous that the Society had a number of ex-Bagnall employees amongst their numbers including T. D. Allen Civil, a well known "Bagnall expert" who later became the Society's Chief Engineer.

One of the first tasks to be carried out was to collect all the various components together and to make an accurate assessment of the work required, it soon became obvious that restoration needed to start again from scratch in order to eliminate some of the previous unsatisfactory work. The Council Depot at Lammascote Road, near the centre of Stafford proved to be an excellent workshop with frequent working parties visiting the site.

It was agreed from the outset that ISABEL should be restored as closely as possible to her condition when she left Castle Engine Works in 1897 and to this end the restoration was carried out to a very high standard.

This is not the place for a blow-by-blow account of the work carried out, but suffice it to say that the Society provided a new all-riveted saddle tank (the welded example produced by Martin Smythe was sold to the Narrow Gauge Railway Society for use on PETER), a new chimney was cast using the patched up original as a pattern, extensive work to the running gear, new cab platework, new non-ferrous fittings, finally being completed with a superb paint job in traditional

On 13 October 1990, the completed ISABEL was displayed on a low loader in the Market Square, Stafford in connection with a book launch. Collection: David H. Smith.

Bagnall style of medium green lined out in red, black and yellow. One or two minor departures were made with the fitting of a steam brake, mechanical lubricator, and eventually, an air brake system for the train, but these did little to detract from the finished locomotive.

The workmanship was such that the Society not only gained the 1989 Dorothea Award for Industrial Conservation, but also the 1993 Steam Heritage Award in the Locomotive category. The resultant prize money contributed towards, in the first instance, a new saddle tank, and in the second a steam/air compressor of the Westinghouse type for the train brake.

Restoration had reached the stage where the locomotive was successfully steam tested in December 1989, following which various minor jobs were completed. Because it was felt that ISABEL had been out of the public gaze for too long, on 13 October 1990, she returned to be displayed in Stafford for the day, in conjunction with the launch of a new book on Bagnall locomotives by Allen Civil and Allan Baker. She took up a position on a trailer in Stafford Market Square, where she created a considerable amount of interest with the Saturday shoppers!

Meantime, progress had been made on building a permanent home for the restored locomotive. This was at Amerton Farm, Stowe-by-Chartley, some 5 miles from Stafford, where the Borough Council was creating a working farm and rare breed centre. A working railway would be an added attraction as well solving the problem of where to house ISABEL. The sod cutting ceremony of the 400 yard long Amerton Railway was held in May 1990, and the first locomotive to arrive, in March 1991, was the ex-Minworth Sewage Works Motor Rail "Simplex"

4w diesel No. 40SD501, following mechanical attention in Tamworth. Two other diesel locomotives (Motor Rail 7471 and Baguley 3024) arrived during 1991, followed by ISABEL itself on 26 October 1991, where she ran in steam for the first time in over 45 years on 27 December 1991, a great occasion indeed.

The public opening of the Amerton Farm Railway was on Sunday 19 July 1992, and the pattern of operations became established; diesel during the week with ISABEL in steam every Sunday, bringing pleasure to young and old, especially to all Stafford residents who remember her on the plinth and "wondered what had happened to her!". During the first full season, March to October 1993, 13,000 passengers were carried.

Although ISABEL usually operates in its Cliffe Hill condition without a cab, a Bagnall-style roof on columns is available for use in inclement weather. Furthermore, an air brakes system has been fitted to comply with modern safety requirements.

In operation, ISABEL has proved very successful, perhaps one drawback is that due to the design of the boiler and firebox (Bagnall's bull-head type) she takes about three and a half hours to raise steam. However, this is more than compensated for when pressure is up and she will steam beautifully all day on 2 cwt. of coal! Perhaps this explains why Cliffe Hill tried a conventional locomotive type boiler before reverting to the bull-head type.

The Society recently carried out an extensive overhaul of the valve gear which was one of the last jobs to be carried out as part of the restoration. ISABEL is the only locomotive in Britain to carry Baguley's Patent Valve Gear which is a most intriguing gear to see in operation, but extremely difficult to set! At the time of writing she was slightly off-beat in forward gear but perfect in reverse!, needless to say investigation is underway to rectify this. The "Modified Baguley" valve gear fitted to SEA LION (Groudle Glen Railway) and RISHRA (Leighton Buzzard Railway) is very different, despite sharing the same designer!

1997 sees ISABEL celebrating her Centenary, one of an increasing number of narrow gauge locomotives to do so, but amongst only a handful of Bagnalls to reach this mark, certainly in this country. The fact that she will also see the year through in full working order is a tribute to the generations of locomen, apprentices and more latterly the members of the Society that have cared for and maintained her over all those years. Long may they do so!